THE ZEALOTS
OF MASADA

BY **MOSHE PEARLMAN**

CHARLES SCRIBNER'S SONS · NEW YORK

THE ZEALOTS OF MASADA

STORY OF A DIG

For my account of the recent excavations, I wish to acknowledge my considerable debt to Professor Yigael Yadin's MASADA: Herod's Fortress and the Zealots' Last Stand, *Random House, Inc., New York, 1966. I must also thank the publishers for their kind permission to quote therefrom.* M.P.

All quotations from Yigael Yadin are taken from MASADA: *Herod's Fortress and the Zealots' Last Stand,* by Yigael Yadin. © Copyright 1966 by Yigael Yadin. Reprinted by permission of Random House, Inc.

Photographs on pages 5, 45, 79, 85, 88, 113, 115, 116, 118, 131, 134, 149, 153, 167, 202, and 206 by courtesy of the Masada Archaeology Expedition and UPI.

Photograph on page 19 by courtesy of the Israel Information Services.

Photographs on front of jacket, title page and pages 9, 41, 59, 62, 89, 94, 107, 111, 120, 121, 138, 139, 146, 150, 152, 156, 157, 159, 165, 166, 169, 170, 176, 198, and 199 by courtesy of the Israel National Parks Authority.

Photographs on pages 13, 50, 63, 77, 104, 110, 117, 126, 161, 172, and 201 by courtesy of the Masada Archaeology Expedition.

Photographs on back of jacket and pages 67 and 98 by courtesy of Kaminer Eliahu and the Israel National Parks Authority.

Printed in the United States of America
Library of Congress Catalog Card Number 67-23691

CONTENTS

1425371

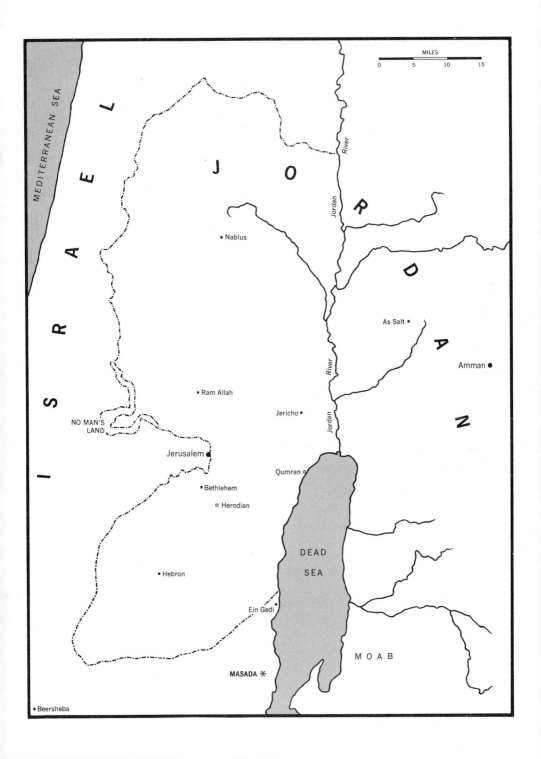

PART I · THE DIG

1 · THE STORY

The time is late March 1965. The place is somewhere in Israel.

On the top of a huge rock, a girl of twenty, an artist from England, in a light cotton blouse and gay shorts, crouches by a shallow trench, carefully scraping away the earth and sifting it with her fingers. Near her, a twenty-two-year-old Israeli farmer is brushing the dirt off what looks like a small green metal object which he has just scooped out of the ground. Behind them are a middle-aged couple from France—he is a taxi driver—putting what appear to be old bits of crockery into a plastic pail. There is a tag on the pail marked with the number of the trench where the pieces of pottery were found.

Above, a hot sun blazes out of a bright clear sky. If they look up from their work, they can see a stretch of glistening blue water, backed by a tall range of reddish mountains. But they do not look up often, and though they are sticky and tired, they seem not to mind. There is energy in their movement and eagerness in their eyes. These people are engaged in a fascinating activity—one which combines the excitement of study with the adventure of a treasure hunt. They are digging up the past.

After a while, a familiar shadow falls across the floor of their trench, and then they do look up. They see a man in his late forties, with a bronzed face, wearing old slacks, an open shirt, and a floppy broad-brimmed sombrero on his balding head, puffing a pipe, and sporting a shooting stick, which he now opens and sits on.

"Anything?" he asks with a large smile.

The young Israeli opens a cardboard box in which he has placed the green object he found, extracts it, and hands it up. The man jumps off his shooting stick, bends forward to take it, and excitedly begins rubbing the metal. Soon he gives an exclamation of joy.

"Do you see what it is?" he asks his friends. "Do you see the date?"

The Israeli does, but the others do not, of course, for they cannot read Hebrew; but the man does not wait for an answer. He has not really asked them. He has just been thinking aloud. He goes on, as much to himself as to them, and cries, "Shekel of Israel. *Jerusalem the Holy. Year Two.* The second year of the Jewish revolt. This is wonderful." He grasps the young farmer by the hand which he pumps up and down in congratulation, and then explains to the others the importance of the find.

The man is Professor Yigael Yadin, leader of the archaeological expedition. The girl and the French couple are some of the many hundreds of men and women from twenty-eight countries who have left their normal labors for a few weeks and volunteered to come here and dig. The Israeli has done the same. And the place—the place which has attracted so many from such distant homes—is the rock of Masada, overlooking the Dead Sea, the remarkable site of a most dramatic event which occurred nineteen hundred years ago.

For the circumstances of that event, we must go back to the

Professor Yigael Yadin joins dig volunteers working on the southwest perimeter of Masada.

time it happened, the first century A.D. The country, the land of the Jews, known at the time as Judea, was then one of the provinces of the great Roman Empire. It had been conquered in the middle of the previous century and ruled since then by Rome.

The governor of the country was appointed by, and answerable to, the Roman emperor. Sometimes he bore the title of king, sometimes of procurator, like Pontius Pilate, who was procurator of Judea at the time of Jesus. The governor had a large force of Roman soldiers—the celebrated Roman legions—to keep order among the population. For the people were not happy to have their freedom crushed, their land occupied by foreign troops, their lives and religion regulated by foreign rulers. They often rebelled, but the rebellions were harshly suppressed.

Yet each clash with the Roman authorities and every fresh wave of Roman cruelty only made the Jews more determined to regain their freedom. Then, in A.D. 66, the Jews throughout the country rose as one man to drive the Romans from their soil. This was the start of what became known in history as the Great Jewish War against the Romans.

At first the Jews made great gains, and Rome soon realized that she was in danger of losing this prized province. She feared that if she did, she would soon lose other important parts of her empire. So she decided to send in her most famous general, Vespasian, who had distinguished himself as commander of the Second Legion in the conquest of Britain, and a large number of additional troops. Even so, the Romans had to fight for every inch of ground, and it took them five years to subdue the country.

The end—they thought—came with their conquest of Jerusalem, the capital, and the destruction of the Jewish Temple. The Temple, which had been built by King Solomon a thousand years before, in the tenth century B.C., was the holiest Jewish shrine. Its destruction was felt by every Jew to be the greatest tragedy that had befallen his people. To this day, Jews throughout the world mark the anniversary by fasting.

Commanding the Roman armies that conquered Jerusalem was Titus, son of Vespasian, who had in the meantime become emperor of Rome. To set an example to others in the Empire who might think of rebelling, Titus slaughtered thousands of Jewish prisoners and took the rest of the captives as slaves to Rome.

But not all. A few managed to escape, and they were determined to continue the fight. They were led by Eleazar ben Ya'ir and were called Zealots. This was because of their "zeal for the Lord," their "zeal for what was right," and, I believe, also because they fought zealously.

Eleazar and his band made their painful way eastward from Jerusalem across the Judean desert. Their sufferings were great. Some had been wounded in the Jerusalem fighting. There was no shelter from the hot sun by day nor the bitter cold at night. They had almost no food and very little water. The sharp rocks over which they had to scramble tore their flesh. They chose this harsh route precisely because they knew they would not be followed by the enemy—certainly not so quickly. They chose it for another reason as well. At the journey's end lay the rock of Masada, and at Masada they believed they could hold out for a long time against the might of Rome.

Masada, they knew, was a natural fortress. In A.D. 66, at the start of the Jewish War, a group of Zealots had attacked the Roman garrison there and captured it. It had remained in Jewish hands. The Romans had never bothered to retake it, both because they thought it would be too costly—it would need too many troops—and because they believed that after the fall of Jerusalem all Jewish resistance would end. They had not reckoned with Eleazar ben Ya'ir.

As soon as he arrived with his party, he set about organizing Masada as a military outpost. With the rock fortress as his base, it was his intention to descend with his men from time to time to make forays against the Romans and against settlers in the region who collaborated with the Romans. If the Romans, goaded by his raids, marched on Masada and tried to capture it, they would find the Jews there holding firm, prepared to make a final stand.

What was there about Masada to give Eleazar such confidence?

It is, as we have said, a natural fortress, a huge rock sticking out from the eastern edge of the Judean plateau, with a sheer drop on all sides. Its flat top, 1,300 feet above the shore of the Dead Sea, is shaped like a diamond. It measures 1,950 feet from its northern to its southern points and 650 feet from east to west. It is very difficult indeed to climb to the top, but it is possible from two sides: one way is along the "snake path," on the sharp eastern slope, so called because, as described by that unusual man, the first century A.D. historian Josephus, it has "the narrowness and constant windings" of a snake. Writing about the actual climb, Josephus said, "Walking along it is like balancing on a tightrope. The least slip means death; for on either side yawns an abyss so terrifying that it could make the boldest tremble." The other approach is from the west, along a spur which meets the side of the fortress at some distance from the top. From there one has to pick one's way upward over a series of dangerous, winding goat paths. Nature has indeed provided excellent defenses for those occupying Masada's summit. Eleazar knew all this. He also knew that about one hundred years before, someone had improved upon nature and powerfully strengthened Masada's defenses. That "someone," now dead some seventy years, was a man whose memory Eleazar despised, because throughout his life he had fawned upon the Romans. It was ironic that this man's fortifications, built with Roman consent, would now serve him, Eleazar, and his Zealots in resisting the Romans. The man was King Herod, "Herod the Great."

Aerial shot of Masada taken from the west. In the distance the mountains of Moab. Below them the Dead Sea. Foreground, the well-preserved Roman ramp, built on the "White Cliff," rising on the western slope of Masada till it appears almost to reach the summit.

He had been a remarkable man, at times brilliant, at times mad, ambitious, cruel, moody; but he had had one constructive passion in life—building. He had built many great cities in the country, the best known being Caesarea, on the Mediterranean coast. Undoubtedly his most spectacular buildings, however, were those he put up on Masada.

Eleazar probably did not know—and certainly did not care— why Herod had spent so much time, money, and energy on fortifying so distant an outpost as Masada. All he was concerned with was the fact that it had been done. But since we shall be writing a good deal about Herod's work on Masada when we come to the discoveries of the Yadin expedition, it is worth interrupting our story to find out what Herod's reasons were.

Herod's family were originally Edomites, inhabitants of Idumea, which bordered on the south of Judea. There had been constant enmity between the Jews and the Edomites, and at the end of the second century B.C., Idumea had been conquered by the Jewish State and became part of Judea. Some years later, Herod's grandfather, who was converted to Judaism, was appointed governor of his native province by the Jewish king and became a man of influence. His son, Herod's father, succeeded to this position of influence, and he retained it after the Romans conquered Judea, under Pompey, in 63 B.C. He was a man who always knew how to keep on the right side of whoever was in power—and so did his son, Herod, who in the meantime had become governor of Galilee.

When his father died, in 43 B.C., Herod took over his authority in the State and was soon busily at work gaining the favor of the Romans. He hoped they would make him king of Judea. But the Romans were in a difficult position. On the one hand, they would have liked to put Herod on the throne, for he was their friend and was "reliable." But precisely because of this, even though he was formally a Jew, he did not have the support of the population, the Jews, and the Romans feared there would be unrest. On the other hand, the person whom the Jews wanted was someone who, like themselves, was anti-Roman. He was Antigonus, a member of the greatly loved Jewish royal family, the Maccabees, who had led the successful fight for Jewish freedom in the middle of the second century B.C.

In the year 40 B.C., the choice was taken out of the hands of Rome when the Jews, aided by the Parthians, drove the Romans from Jerusalem. Antigonus was crowned king. Herod had lost the struggle for power, and he promptly fled—to Masada!

It was while he was sitting on top of Masada with his household and some eight hundred followers that Herod became deeply impressed with the defense possibilities of the rock. However, he had no intention of staying there all his life. He still wanted to be king. Leaving his younger brother in charge at Masada, he made his way to Rome. There he was eventually able to persuade the authorities to give him their support as the only way of regaining their power in Judea. The Roman Senate nominated him puppet king and sent him back to Judea with two Roman legions—a powerful force. In the year 37 B.C., after a five months' siege, Jerusalem was taken and Antigonus put to death. Herod was enthroned in his place.

What had happened to his followers in Masada while he was away? To his surprise, Herod found that they had been able to hold out all that time, although they had been attacked often. This showed what a useful refuge Masada was, and could be, if he ever needed one; and when he thought of his situation, he thought he might. True, he was on the throne; but the throne was shaky. He faced two dangers. One was from his subjects, the Jews. They hated him, for he was the puppet of their enemy, and would have loved nothing better than to push him off and restore one of their beloved Maccabees. The second danger came from a well-known lady who reigned in Egypt at the time—Cleopatra. Cleopatra had her eyes on the kingdom of Judea and wished it annexed to Egypt. She kept appealing to Marc Antony, her great and good friend, who was one of the rulers of the Roman Empire, "begging him," according to Josephus, "to destroy Herod and requesting the transfer to herself of Judea."

In these circumstances, Herod thought it would be a good idea to strengthen the fortifications of Masada and equip it to enable him to withstand a long siege. The orders he must have given to his architects and engineers were to put up buildings and install facilities "fit for a king"—in the event that he would have to live there in refuge for a long time. When Eleazar ben Ya'ir, more than one hundred years later, reached Masada with his bedraggled followers, bleeding, footsore, and hungry, what they saw matched in richness what they had heard.

Within a defense wall encircling the top of the rock, they saw palaces, Roman baths, storerooms, water cisterns, and aqueducts—an amazing collection of buildings on the top of a lonely cliff in the middle of nowhere.

Herod never had to use it as a refuge. He reigned from 37 B.C. until his death in 4 B.C.; but he must have visited Masada often. When he did, it is unlikely that he ever dreamed, in the words of Josephus, "that he was to leave it to the Romans as their very last task in the war against the Jews."

The buildings themselves may have been luxurious, but to Eleazar and his frugal Zealots they were a symbol of all they despised—ostentation, personal comfort, personal ambition, personal power. However, what had served one man, his household, and a small garrison would now be used to serve the community of Zealots, the few hundred families who had escaped from Jerusalem and the few who had been at Masada

Aerial view of Masada summit showing excavations of Herodian buildings.

all the time. The storehouses and water cisterns would be most useful; indeed, they would enable them to hold out for a long time. As for the palaces and other buildings, they would be used to house a number of families. Additional shelter would be offered by the rooms in the wall that Herod had built around the perimeter. This was what is known as the casemate type, a double wall with space in between which is divided into chambers, or casemates. What the Zealots would do therefore would be to use these rooms as family dwellings. They would also, in time, build several primitive shacks as additional housing.

All through the rest of A.D. 70, 71, and the first part of 72, the Zealots continued to occupy Masada and harry the Roman authorities whenever they could, as well as disrupt Roman rule in the area. At first the Romans paid little attention to them, dismissing them as a mild nuisance, ignoring them as one would a gnat. But as the Zealot raids continued, the gnat became a bee and then a wasp with a painful sting, and the Romans began to take notice. "Who are these people?" the Romans asked themselves. "Don't they know when they are beaten? Don't they know that with Jerusalem lost and the rest of the country under firm Roman rule they don't have a chance?"

What annoyed the Romans even more than their losses in the Zealot raids was the harm to their prestige—the prestige of the great Roman Empire. How could the local Roman governor and commander face their imperial masters when they seemed unable to put down a small group of Judean rebels? But how *could* they be put down? A large force was necessary, and such a force was not available to the Romans in the first year or so when they were busily trying to establish order in the country after the long savage war.

In A.D. 72, however, the new Roman procurator of Judea, Flavius Silva, considered that the country was now quiet and the population sufficiently terrorized into acceptance of

Roman rule. He decided that the time had come to move against the one fortress that still held out—Masada. It is also possible that he got direct instructions from Rome to do so.

Flavius Silva was a general. He had been one of the top commanders of Titus in the conquest of Jerusalem. Cruel he may have been, but he was a first class military man, and he did not underrate the enemy. He knew it would not be easy to take the high rock, particularly if it were defended by Zealots, whom he knew from Jerusalem to be stubborn and courageous fighters. He decided to march on Masada with a large force—and to lead them himself, for he could not afford a Roman failure. Such a failure would not only be a blow to Roman prestige but might also have the effect of exciting similar rebellious outbreaks in the rest of the country, and the war against Rome would begin all over again.

He had to make certain of victory, so he took the noted Tenth Legion and additional troops—from 6,000 to 10,000 fighters in all—to subdue the thousand or so Masada defenders. It was quite a compliment to Eleazar ben Ya'ir. In addition to his fighting men, General Silva also pressed into service from 10,000 to 15,000 "bearers"—prisoners of war—to carry supplies over the long stretch of barren desert. Eleazar's group, which in the end totaled 960 men, women, and children, would be facing a total enemy force of not less than 16,000 and possibly as great as 25,000!

After months of preparation, Silva set out across the wilderness with his massive force. The journey alone must have taken them several weeks, and the stores they carried must have been enormous. They would find no water on the way, so they would have had to take with them every drop they would need during the journey, as well as reserves for the initial period after their arrival. The same was true with food and wood. The problem of supplies for thousands of men—even though the prisoner-slaves would get very little—was staggering. This force would not have set out on such a journey without elaborate preparations, as had Eleazar. Eleazar's band numbered comparatively few, and they were in a hurry and desperate and ready to suffer grave privations of thirst and hunger. But the Roman Army was not—particularly when, with so many prisoner-slaves, it was unnecessary.

Eventually they arrived at the foot of Masada on the shore of the Dead Sea, the lowest habitable spot on earth, 1,200 feet below sea level. General Silva took a good look at the rock he had come to conquer, which loomed 1,300 feet above the level of the shore. We have no record of his thoughts, but he may well have been shaken by the seeming impossibility of scaling the steep heights, with a hostile group on top ready to roll down stones or pour boiling oil upon any who attempted the climb.

As he circled the rock from below, Silva noticed that while the steep sides fell away for all or almost all of the 1,300 feet on the north, the east, and the south, the western side fell sharply only about a fifth of the way. At that point there was the spur we mentioned, a neck of hill or kind of bridge known as the "White Cliff," linking the Masada rock with the broad Judean plateau. It was from this direction that Silva decided to launch his attack, and it was here, near the western slope, that he established his headquarters camp.

The written record does not say whether he tried immediately to storm the fortress. He may well have done so, hoping for a quick victory and expecting that his vast numbers would make up for his topographic disadvantage. But if he did, he failed; for we know both from the record and from the structures he erected that he was forced to lay siege to Masada and build up to a final assault when his men and war machines could get closer to the summit.

He established eight camps at key points around the base of the rock. Their remains may be seen today. Then he set his slaves to building a powerful siege wall, called a circumvallation, completely encircling the fortress. It was more than two miles long (3,800 yards to be exact), and six feet thick. In one section, it was strengthened by twelve towers. He must have built this wall partly to prevent the Zealots from raiding his troops and partly to stop them from escaping. Not that Eleazar had any intention of fleeing, as we shall soon see. But Silva did not know this, and he must have been anxious to kill or capture this stubborn band, which had caused such trouble to him and his Empire, and he did not want anyone to get away.

When all this work was completed, General Silva commenced the final stage of his operation, the purpose for which he had come—the assault on and capture of the heights of Masada. Getting his troops to scramble up the steep sides of the rock had proved a failure. They could not fight and climb at the same time, and they certainly could not climb with heavy weapons; they formed too easy a target and prey for the defenders on the top. The only way, Silva must have thought, to break through the Zealots' defenses was to build a sloping ramp reaching to the summit. Up this ramp he could move his troops in a solid body, together with siege engines and a battering ram, and hurl this powerful strength against a single point in the Zealots' casemate wall. It would mean hard labor for a lot of men. But he had the prisoner-slaves, and he did not mind how hard they worked. The defenders on the top would of course try to stop the construction. But arrows and catapult stones would force them to keep their heads down and get away from the wall.

Where would it be best to build this ramp? Obviously on the "White Cliff," the western side, close to where he had established his headquarters. From here, the distance to the top of Masada was only about 250 feet, as against the 1,200 or 1,300 feet he would have to bridge if he chose the northern, eastern, or southern slopes.

The Roman general thereupon set his men to building this solid ramp upon the "White Cliff." They piled earth and stones upon it and tamped them down so that the surface was hard. Wooden scaffolding was used to hold the earth in place. To this day you can see the protruding tips of timber. The structure was cone-shaped, narrow at the bottom and broadening to a width of about 650 feet near Masada's wall. That was also its length. This ramp, which is quite well preserved, is regarded as one of the most remarkable siege works of the Romans still in existence.

The ramp did not reach the summit of Masada, possibly because the gradient would have been too steep or perhaps it would have been too difficult and costly in men. At all events, Silva solved that problem by having a pier thrown up on top of the ramp as a base for a high siege tower from which his men could dominate the defenders.

As Josephus says: "Finding that it [the ramp] was not of sufficient strength [and height] to support the [siege] machines, they raised on it a kind of platform, composed of large stones, fifty cubits [75 feet] in height, and of the same breadth. On this platform they built a tower of the height of sixty cubits [90 feet], which they fortified with iron. Exclusive of their common [siege] machines, they had another kind, which had been invented by Vespasian, and were afterwards improved by Titus. From the tower above-mentioned the Romans assailed the besieged with such impetuous showers of stones and flights of arrows that they were afraid to appear on the walls. In the interim Silva directed his battering ram against the wall, till at length it was damaged in some places."

What is evident from Josephus' report is that the Romans on the tower's platform, hurling their stones and arrows among the Zealots, gave what is known as "covering fire" to the men beneath them wielding the "ram." This weapon, so called because of its function of butting, like the ram, was used to make a hole in the defense wall through which the troops could rush. It consisted of a huge length of stout wood, usually the trunk of a large tree, with a metal point at its front

Aerial view of Masada taken from the northwest. The Roman ramp is clearly visible on the right.

end. The more advanced type was housed in a wooden structure and rested on a flexible "cradle" of loops slung from the roof. This was probably the kind of ram used by Silva, and his men would keep swinging it against the wall with all their strength. The thin walls of a casemate would soon crumble. Troops operating the ram were often covered by a leather canopy to protect them from the heavy stones or boiling oil which the defenders above would aim at their heads. At Masada we know that they were protected not only by their companions on the tower but also by catapult throwers firing from small platforms above the roof of their own ram structure.

It is not hard to imagine the scene among the Zealots when their wall was breached, although from the way they reacted at the time, and from what happened later, we know they did not panic. For months they had been watching the Roman build-up. They could follow every step. They could hear almost every sound. (The acoustics in the area are unusually clear. Some months ago I stood on the western section of the casemate wall, and a friend stood below in the middle of Silva's camp, and we spoke to each other. Neither of us had to shout too loudly to be heard distinctly by the other. Thus, at the time of the siege, might Eleazar's band have heard the curses of Silva's soldiers, and they the jeers of the defenders.) They had observed the arrival of the Roman forces, the setting-up of their camps, the building of the siege wall—and finally the construction of the ramp. They knew what was coming. They had, throughout that time, been subjected to constant "fire" by the missiles of the Romans. From the very first they had kept a day and night vigil all around their casemate wall to prevent the Romans from scaling the heights; and as we shall see when we deal with the discoveries of the recent expedition, they had kept piles of ammunition—stone balls—at key points along the wall to fling at anyone trying to do so. Along the western section of the perimeter, their guards were strengthened. It was clear to them from the Roman preparations that this was where Silva would strike; but just in case the Roman activity was a ruse, a feint to mislead them, they kept a watchful eye all around. Being pitifully few in number, made daily fewer by the Roman missiles, the male Zealots were the fighters manning the defenses while the women and older children carried the ammunition, rushed messages from one sector to the other, tended the wounded, cooked the meager rations, and drew and distributed the water.

We can gather from the evidence that up to the final days they were hopeful that they might hold out. Despite their fearful hardships, their morale was high. As month followed month and they saw that the Romans assembled below were apparently powerless to defeat them, they took heart. Their spirits rose at the thought that they, a mere handful, were holding at bay a great Roman army, led by a renowned general. Devoutly religious and familiar with the Bible, some must surely have likened their lot to that of David facing Goliath —except that the Roman Goliath was infinitely more powerful.

But when the siege tower was erected and the battering ram brought up, Eleazar and his commanders must certainly have realized that the end could not be far off. Yet they reacted with great coolness. Unable to keep the ram from the wall, because of the arrows and catapult stones from the Romans on the tower, they knew that the casemate would be breached any minute. What did they do? They promptly rushed all hands to the section of the wall that was now crumbling and improvised an inner wall. This was one which could be put up quickly yet built in such a way that it would better meet the threat of the battering ram. They erected what was in fact a wooden casemate—two parallel walls made of long wooden beams—except that the space between was not left empty but was filled with earth, and boards were nailed across the frame to prevent the earth from falling out. It was an ingenious answer to the powerful Roman weapon, whose blows, far from causing further damage, simply beat the earth into a more solid and compact barrier.

But General Flavius Silva, an experienced soldier, was also not without ingenuity. Like Eleazar, he too remained the cool commander when things went wrong, although it was far easier for him to do so; and things were going wrong for him now. He was finding that the great weapon on which he had pinned his hopes, the weapon that had actually breached the wall, was now powerless.

Only a little while earlier, when he had been told that the wall was about to crumble, he had imagined his men rushing through the gap and at last, at last, grappling with the enemy. This was the moment he had waited for, the moment for which he had pushed and spurred his men for long weary months to build the camps and the siege wall and the towers and the great ramp—the moment when he would get at the enemy. We can imagine him as he watches and waits near the foot of the ramp, expecting every moment the report from the top that the ram has done its job, the wall has been pierced and his men are through. He has already received the first news about the breach. Then nothing. The minutes tick by, and still there is no movement of his men onto the summit. We can see him impatiently sending an aide to find out what is holding them up and the aide returning to say that they have struck a snag. He then strides up the ramp to see for himself, and he sees the new defense construction of the Zealots.

After his initial disappointment and after examining the new wall from where he stood, Silva quickly must have decided what to do. He would strike at its one weakness—the timber. He ordered his men to get firebrands—flaming torches —and hurl them at the new barrier. They did, and the wood soon caught fire. Within moments, the whole section was ablaze.

Then there occurred a remarkable and unusual event. The Roman Silva was too experienced a commander not to have thought about the wind before giving the order to set fire to the enemy wall. From his point of view, the wind was blowing in the right direction—toward the Masada summit, carrying the flames with it. But suddenly the wind veered around, blowing the flames back in the faces of the Romans and threatening to set alight their siege tower and battering ram.

Josephus tells us that this strange happening "plunged the Romans into despair." We can well imagine that the hopes of the Jewish Zealots on the other side, only a few yards away, must have risen anew. Indeed, when we think of the momentous hours of that day so long ago—the year was now A.D. 73—we are struck by the fast succession of ups and downs experienced by both sides. Eleazar's joy was Silva's gloom, and Roman despair was Zealot hope. Now, with the change of wind, the defenders must surely have thought that Providence had come to their rescue at the last minute.

But hope died quickly—as quickly as the wind again veered and resumed its former direction, carrying and flinging the flames against the wall, turning it, according to Josephus, into one solid blazing mass. (During the recent expedition, the archaeologists occasionally experienced this freak phenomenon, when the prevailing wind would suddenly turn on itself for a few moments and as suddenly veer back again.)

Then, says Josephus, "the Romans returned to their camp full of spirits, and with a fixed determination to attack the enemy by break of day on the following morning; and, in the meantime, to place strong guards, that their opponents might not escape in the night."

But the Jewish Zealot leader, Eleazar ben Ya'ir, had no thought of escaping—at least not in the way the Romans thought. He knew, though, that the moment of greatest crisis had come. The banging of the battering ram had stopped. No more stones and arrows were being flung from the siege tower. He had heard the heavy tread of the Roman troops as they marched down the ramp, and he had heard their jeers as they went. "See you in the morning," they had cried, taunting the Zealots, and Eleazar knew what that meant. With the stone wall breached and the wooden wall burning, nothing now stood between his small group and their meager weapons and the full might of Silva's army. When the Romans returned to the attack in the morning, pouring through the gap in the defenses to engage the Zealots in direct combat, their sheer weight of numbers and the power of their weapons would prove more than a match for the defenders. Even if every Zealot fighter battled to the end, selling his life dearly, the outcome could not be in doubt. Then would follow the slaughter of the survivors or, worse, torture and captivity. He could envisage the women and children dragged in chains through the streets of Judea and then probably Rome, as an example of what happened to people who dared defy Roman authority; and they would end their days in slavery.

These were the thoughts in Eleazar's mind as he stood, sad and lonely, watching the flames devour the improvised wall. Sad not over the life he had led nor the brave fight he had fought but over the way it was now ending—in Roman victory and not in Jewish freedom. Sad, above all, that God had abandoned them. Lonely, because in moments of great decision, every commander is lonely. He knew now what that decision must be. From the way he had reasoned, only two courses were open to him: surrender or death. General Silva, as soon as the ramp was completed, had called upon him to surrender. Both forces, as we have seen, were within calling distance of each other, and the Romans, when they were not firing at the Zealots, were shouting to them, "Give up. You don't have a chance. Surrender." But the Zealots had either remained silent or rejected the calls with contempt. Now, just after the firebrands had done their work and just before the Romans had left the ramp, they had again cried out to the defenders to give in. When this had been spurned, they had marched off with their gloating promise of a rendezvous in the morning.

Surrender, then, was out of the question. There remained only—death. With this resolution in his mind, Eleazar assembled his comrades and delivered what may well be one of the most dramatic addresses in history, the more moving when one pictures the circumstances. It was related by the only survivors—two women and five children who failed to go through with Eleazar's plan and hid themselves. It has been preserved for us in the writings of Josephus.

These were the words of Eleazar ben Ya'ir on that fateful night on the top of Masada, uttered in the glow of the blazing wall:

It has been, my friends, the usual custom with the people of our nation, to deny the authority of every other lord than the great Sovereign of the universe, the eternal God; and this we have done without excepting the Romans or anyone else. The time has now come when we must demonstrate our sincerity by our conduct; wherefore let us act like men of resolution.

Till this time we have run every risk in preservation of our freedom; but we must now expect thralldom and tormenting punishments if the enemy take us alive, since we first departed from their dominion and have been the last to resist them. This being the case, we may deem it a favor if we are permitted to choose the death we would die, a favor that has been refused to many of our people.

We shall all be made slaves tomorrow if we obtain not our liberty this night. But this we may do in a way that our enemies cannot prevent. The utmost of their ambition is to make us prisoners, and it is in vain to struggle against them any longer . . . for Providence hath decreed our destruction. The wind and the fire that combined to destroy our new wall furnish a proof of the justice of this observation; for you cannot think but the sudden turning of this wind was intended as a punishment of the crimes of which we have been guilty toward each other. Admitting, then, that our punishment is at once just and inevitable, what remains but that we rather execute justice on ourselves, than leave it to the victorious Romans to pour down on us the vengeance of Heaven. Thus acting, we should secure the honor of our wives and protect our children from slavery. Let us . . . make our own terms and die free. But let us first set fire to the fortress and to our possessions; and thus the Romans, neither taking us prisoners nor finding anything to loot, will even regret the possession of the place. One thing only let us spare—our store of food: to serve as a proof that we were not driven to this violent procedure by famine, but maintained our first resolution of dying rather than submitting to slavery.

Not all responded in the same way to Eleazar's appeal. "Some," says Josephus, "were eager to do as he said, deeming death an object of desire in their present situation; while others, from the tenderness of their nature, were moved by pity for their wives and families, and certainly, too, by the prospect of becoming their own executioners. And as they exchanged glances, the tears in their eyes betrayed the sentiments of their minds." So Eleazar, "addressing himself particularly, and with the utmost earnestness, to those who were weeping," went on:

. . . Will anyone who is not destitute of the common spirit of man wish to view the rising of another sun? Nay, would he wish it even if he might live in safety? Can anyone have so little regard to his country, so mean, so contracted a soul, as not to regret that he has survived to behold this fatal day? Happy would it have been for us if we had all been sacrificed, rather than to have witnessed this sacrilegious destruction and to have beheld Jerusalem itself become a pile of ruins.

While hope remained, however, our courage did not fail, and we despaired not of a happy change in our affairs. But as we have now no further reason to expect so auspicious a circumstance, and as we are urged by an invincible necessity to the step we ought now to take, it becomes us to have regard to our wives, our children, and ourselves; and in the plan of our proceeding we should be expeditious, while the means are yet in our power.

All men are equally destined to death; and the same fate attends the coward as the brave. But outrage, slavery, and the sight of our wives led away to shame with our children—these are not evils to which man is subject by the laws of nature: men undergo them through their own cowardice if they have the chance to forestall them by death and will not take it.

We had courage to abandon the Romans, to defy those who called themselves our masters, to reject their offer, now, in the final stages, to spare our lives. Will anyone think that these circumstances will be forgotten if they should take us prisoner?

It is a melancholy reflection to consider the situation of our old people or our youth when we are subjected. The former will die beneath their torments, and the latter languish under them while strength remains. The husband must expect to be an eye-witness of the dishonor of his wife, and the parent to behold his children begging for relief from their chains.

Yet, while freedom is our own, and we are in possession of our swords, let us make a determined use of them to preserve our liberties. Let us die free men, gloriously surrounded by our wives and children. And let us be expeditious. Eternal renown shall be ours by snatching the prize from the hands of our enemies, and leaving them nothing to triumph over but the bodies of those who dared to be their own executioners.

Thus spoke Eleazar. Now the response was unanimous. "Eleazar," says Josephus, "had many more arguments to urge, but that the people interrupted him with the warmest expressions of their readiness to adopt the plan he had recommended." So long as there was hope, they had fought, believing, too, that they were the instrument of God's will, through whom the Romans would be conquered and Jewish freedom regained. But now, with disaster inevitable, it was clear that the will of God was the reverse of what they had hoped, and death was welcomed. They had little time left, and they moved quickly to do the grim thing that they had to do.

What happened next is related in moving words by Josephus. This is strange, for as we shall see later, Josephus was thoroughly hated—and with good reason—by the Zealots, and he hated them with equal passion. He was a man who wished to find favor in the eyes of his masters in Rome, and all his writings were pro-Roman. Yet he must have been so impressed by the behavior of Eleazar's group that in describing this episode at Masada he was unable to suppress his admiration for their strength of character—so different from his own. This is what he says:

Thus passionately were these people devoted to the destruction of themselves and their families! It was very extraordinary that, when they came to give proof of their resolution, not a man of them failed in the arduous trial. They retained their kindest affections for each other to the last moment, conceiving that they could not render a more acceptable proof of their regard.

Now came the deed.

While they embraced their wives and children for the last time, they wept over and stabbed them in the same moment, taking comfort, however, that this work was not to be performed by their enemies. They considered the necessity of the action as their excuse, and reflected that they only destroyed their dearest friends to prevent their falling by the hands of the Romans. In a word, there was not one man wanting in the necessary courage on the occasion. . . .

Those who had been the principal agents in this slaughter, penetrated as they were with grief for the necessity, resolved not to survive those they had slain, and immediately collecting all their effects together, they set them on fire. This being done, they cast lots for the selection of ten men out of their number to destroy the rest.

Josephus continues:

These being chosen, the devoted victims embraced the bodies of their deceased families, and then, ranging themselves near them, cheerfully resigned themselves to the hands of the executioners. When these ten men had discharged their disagreeable task, they again cast lots as to which of the ten should kill the other nine, and last of all himself: so great was the trust that these people reposed in each other that neither in doing nor in suffering should one differ from another.

The nine devoted victims died with the same resolution as their brethren had done. And the surviving man, having surveyed the bodies in case amidst all the slaughter someone was still left in need of his hand, threw himself on his sword, among his companions, but not till he had first set fire to the palace.

The deceased had imagined that not a single Jew would fall into the hands of the Romans. But it afterwards appeared that an old woman and another woman who was related to Eleazar, in intelligence and education superior to most women, together with five children, had escaped. They had hidden in the conduits that brought drinking water underground. Including women and children, no less than nine hundred and sixty persons were slain on this occasion. This melancholy scene happened on the fifteenth day of the month Xanthicus [April].

On the dawn of the following morning, the Romans prepared their scaling ladders [to bridge the gap between the pier on the ramp and the summit of Masada], in order to make an attack. But they were astonished in the highest degree on not hearing any noise but the crackling of the flames and were totally at a loss what conjecture to form. On this they gave a loud shout, as if giving the signal for a volley, in expectation of receiving an answer. This noise alarmed the women in their place of retreat, who immediately coming out related the truth to the Romans as it really happened, the second of them providing a lucid report of Eleazar's speech and the action that had followed. The story, however, appeared so extraordinary that they could not give credit to it; but they exerted themselves in extinguishing the fire. And being employed in this service till they came to the palace, they there found the bodies of the deceased lying in heaps.

Far, however, from exulting in the triumph of joy that might have been expected from enemies, they united to admire the steady virtue and dignity of mind with which the Jews had been inspired, and wondered at that generous contempt of death by which such numbers had been bound in one solemn compact.

This, then, is the story of Masada as it has come down to us

from the writings of Josephus. This was the drama that inspired Dr. Yigael Yadin, Professor of Archaeology at the
Hebrew University, Jerusalem, to carry out a thorough excavation of the site.

Archaeology is defined in the dictionary as the study of
antiquities. It is perhaps simpler to think of it as exploring the
ruins of the distant past. History is also a study of the past, but
the historian can sit in a comfortable chair at his desk in his
home or in a library and try and work out what happened by
reading records of the period which interests him. The archaeologist also consults the written records. But then he goes out
to the place where the happenings occurred, starts digging, or
excavating, as it is called, looking for ruins or objects which
the people of old left behind. Then, by careful study of what
he finds, he can form a picture of life at the time and re-create
the events that took place. Archaeologists can thus tell you,
by examining the ruins and objects of an ancient city, what
people wore two and three and more thousand years ago,
what they ate, what they worked at, what their religion was,
what kind of houses or caves they lived in, how they were
organized, how they fought. If the archaeologist is lucky
enough to find some ancient writing—which can often be
read immediately by a scholar or, if it is unknown, can eventually be deciphered—he can tell what people *thought* at the
time and a lot of other things.

An archaeologist may be interested in a place about which
there are written records—like Masada and the account of
Josephus. What he finds, when he digs, may prove that the
records are true or false and, if true, may add important
knowledge to the record. For example, the Bible tells us that
King Solomon built chariot cities in Hazor, Megiddo, and
Gezer. At a recent archaeological expedition to Hazor and
experimental digs at Megiddo and Gezer (also carried out by
Yigael Yadin), the scholars found the stone gateways and the
walls of these cities, which King Solomon's architects and

engineers had built in the tenth century B.C., nearly three thousand years ago.

Would the Masada story prove true or false? If true, would the Yadin expedition find physical evidence of the dramatic end? Would they find the skeletons of the Zealots? Would they find the ashes of the fires they lit under their possessions? Would there be arrowheads and ammunition of balls of stone which the Romans had hurled in their midst throughout the siege? Would they find any food left in the storehouses as Eleazar had instructed? Would they find clues as to how the Zealots lived?

Most important of all, perhaps, was the question in Yadin's mind as to whether they would find scrolls or other written documents left by the Zealots. The Zealots were deeply religious people, very orthodox Jews, and they were bound to have had with them sacred writings—handwritten scrolls of books of the Bible, prayers, and other religious documents. It is unlikely that they would have allowed their sacred works to fall into the hands of the Roman pagans, and they may well have buried them before they took their lives. If they had remained untouched since then, they were probably in a good state of preservation. For the climate in the Dead Sea area is hot and dry, and untouched objects may be preserved for many centuries. Masada, after all, is less than thirty miles from the caves of Qumran where the famous Dead Sea Scrolls were found. Biblical documents belonging to the Zealots, if found, would be of the greatest historical interest. They would be perhaps the most ancient such documents in existence; and unlike other ancient biblical scrolls, these could be dated accurately and positively as belonging to not later than A.D. 73!

Indeed, any object found among the Zealots' remains—if the story were found to be true—would enjoy this great and rare advantage over finds in most other archaeological digs: accurate dating. This would also help to date similar objects found at other archaeological sites in the region—pottery, pieces of cloth, weapons, style of building, and so on. Giving an accurate date to a discovery is one of the most important and difficult aims of the archaeologist.

But if the Zealot's story was what drew Yadin to Masada, once he was excavating his area of interest would be much wider. He would try to find and study the ruins of all the buildings erected by Herod and so contribute much to our knowledge of Roman-style architecture and building techniques in the first century B.C.

Had Herod been the first to fortify Masada? Josephus said some fortification work had been done by "Jonathan the High Priest." Which Jonathan did he mean? Most scholars held that it had been Jonathan Maccabeus (brother of the great Judah the Maccabee) who was head of the Jewish Commonwealth in the middle of the second century B.C. But it might have been Alexander Jannai, (Jonathan Maccabeus' great-nephew), the Jewish king who reigned at the beginning of the first century B.C. and was also known as "Jonathan the High Priest." This was another of the archaeological problems Yadin's expedition would try to solve.

A word now about the man whose report kept alive the story of Masada—Josephus Flavius. If it were not for him, history might never have known of the last Jewish stand against the Romans. The story of the Zealots would have died with them.

Josephus was a Jew, born in Judea in A.D. 37, who rose to high positions in the Jewish State and then betrayed his own people, going over to the Romans. His given name was Yoseph ben Matatyahu and he adopted the Josephus Flavius after his act of betrayal. As a young man he studied Jewish law and was apparently a very bright student. He then became a priest. In A.D. 64, seeking, it was said, to right a wrong that had been done by the Roman authorities in the country against some of his friends, who were also priests, he visited Rome. There he managed to become acquainted with the empress, the wife of Nero, and through her got to know some of the Romans in high positions.

Returning to Judea, he found his countrymen boiling with revolt against the tyrannical authority of the local Roman administration. As one who had just come back from Rome, and impressed with the power of the Roman Empire, he is said to have argued against Jewish revolutionary action. He was, of course, not listened to, but his loyalty was not doubted, and after the outbreak of the Jewish rebellion in A.D. 66, he was sent to Galilee as governor in the interests of the Jewish patriot forces.

He was, however, strongly opposed by the local patriots in Galilee, who *did* doubt his reliability, and they urged the heads of the revolt in Jerusalem to recall him. Somehow Josephus managed to reassure Jerusalem, and he remained.

From what Josephus writes about himself—and he wrote much—those who doubted him were right to have done so. For after the Romans began gaining the upper hand in Galilee, he "saw the inevitable end awaiting the Jews and knew that their one safety lay in a change of heart." Speaking of himself in the third person, he says he "felt sure he would be pardoned if he went over to the Romans": but, on the other hand, "he would have died over and over rather than betray his mother-land and flout the trust reposed in him in order to make him-self at home with those he had been sent to fight." However, he wrote this several years after the event, and he may have been trying to justify for posterity his act of betrayal. Actu-ally, when he fought against the Romans, he fought well, and he also trained his soldiers well, trying to organize them into a regular force on the lines of the Roman legions.

With the arrival of Vespasian and his considerable army in A.D. 67, which had been mustered to crush the Jewish revolt, the Jewish cities in Galilee soon began to fall. Josephus was forced to retire from one defense line to the next and finally made a stand at a place called Jotapata, a Galilean mountain stronghold. There he and his men fought valiantly, with great courage and cunning, keeping the Romans at bay for forty-seven days. Vespasian himself, says Josephus, directed the siege and the assaults. With him was his son, Titus. Vespasian knew that he, Josephus, was his opposing commander and that with his capture Jewish resistance in Galilee would collapse.

What a strange man was this Josephus—brilliant lawyer, theologian, administrator, fighter, and writer. He says himself that even while fighting the Romans so fanatically at Jotapata, he was already thinking of a way to join them! The way he eventually found makes even more strange his moving words on the end of Masada. How does he justify himself? By claiming that he was inspired by prophecy, saw that God was punishing the Jewish people and favoring the Romans, "and because Thou didst choose my spirit to make known the things to come, I yield myself willingly to the Romans that I may live, but I solemnly declare that I go, not as a traitor, but as Thy servant."

When Jotapata fell, Josephus managed to escape and hide in a cave with forty other men in the midst of the massacre. Three days later, the Romans detected his hiding place and, writes Josephus, "Vespasian immediately sent two tribunes . . . with orders to offer Josephus safe conduct and persuade him to come out." He wished to, but this shocked his companions, amazed that he should be "so in love with life" that he could "bear to live as a slave," and they threatened to run him through with their swords if he should seek to surrender himself to the Romans rather than "fall upon his own weapon and die in a manner worthy of a general of the Jews."

Then came betrayal by a trick, an episode reminiscent in part of the last night at Masada—although there had been no treachery there. What makes the story so odd is that it is Josephus himself who relates it, and he says openly that he used a "stratagem" to trick his forty companions. Seeing that they were doomed and determined "to destroy themselves rather than become subject to Rome," he won them over by "addressing them in a style of authority, calling one by name, taking another by the hand, endeavouring to engage the attention of the rest by argument and such other means as he conceived to be best adapted for obtaining the end he had in view." He then talked to them of the "horrid guilt of suicide" and suggested a different plan. Instead of taking their own lives, let them cast lots, and then number two would kill number one, number three would kill number two, four would kill three, and so on. This way "we shall avoid self-murder." They agreed, and "either through chance or the care of Providence," Josephus drew the last number! He was thus one of the last two survivors, and not wishing to kill or be killed, he persuaded his destined victim to live. 1425371

Giving himself up, he was brought before Vespasian. Titus was present at the meeting. Josephus amazed the general by saying, "I am authorized by the Almighty to impart to you a matter of the highest importance." That was why he had "submitted to be made a prisoner" rather than "acted consistently with the character of a Jewish general and . . . died." What was this matter? It was a prophecy that Vespasian would become emperor and that his son Titus would rule after him. He suggested that Vespasian hold him in prison, and if the prophecy failed, do with him as he wished.

Vespasian must have been intrigued by this strange approach, for he agreed. Two years later Vespasian became emperor, and Josephus was freed, taken under Vespasian's wing, awarded a pension, made a Roman citizen, and given an estate in Judea.

It was then, at the age of thirty-two, that Josephus began his seven-volume history of *The Wars of the Jews with the*

Romans, to be followed by his twenty-volume *The Antiqui-*
ties of the Jews and numerous other works. I have said earlier
that his books on the Jewish wars are pro-Roman—and also
pro-Josephus. Nevertheless, taking into account his bias and
prejudice, it is possible to understand much of what went on
at that time. Some of it we know from his pen alone—for
example, the story of Masada. What is of added importance
for us and was of great importance to the Yadin archaeological expedition is that Josephus was a most detailed historian.
No fact was too minor for him to mention. Not all his facts
may have been accurate; but a preliminary survey of the
physical features of the rock of Masada showed that most of
his detailed descriptions were correct, and they served as an
excellent guide as to what to dig for and where. Would the
archaeologists also find that his story of the Zealots was true?*

The answer was given just 1900 years after Josephus's
report by another and very different kind of Jewish general,
also "born in Judea"—Professor Yigael Yadin, who had been
Chief of Operations during Israel's War of Liberation in
1948 and subsequently Israel's Chief of Staff before he retired
from the Army to devote himself to archaeology.

---

* For those who would like to read Josephus for themselves, it should
be added that his writings were in Greek. The standard English version
was done by W. Whiston in 1737. There have been several new translations since then, one of the most recent being the 1959 work of G. A.
Williamson, rendered in modern English. The quotations I have used
in this book are taken from the 1794 translation by Charles Clarke,
published in Britain, for Clarke, I feel, has caught the authentic flavor
of antiquity. M. P.

2 · THE PREPARATIONS

Masada was excavated by the Yadin expedition* in two seasons of digging, from October 1963 to May 1964 and from November 1964 to April 1965—eleven months in all. But the first spade touched the ground on the first day of the dig only after many months of careful preparation and the hurdling of tough obstacles.

In planning an archaeological expedition, you have to worry not only about such professional items as drafting paper for drawings of the antiquities but also about such simple yet vital needs as food for the teams, water for drinking and washing, sleeping accommodation. You have to set up a camp; and you have to decide where. Since Masada, like many other archaeological sites, is far from a city, you have to worry

* Officially called the Masada Archaeological Expedition, the dig was carried out on behalf of the Hebrew University of Jerusalem, the Israel Exploration Society, and the Israel Government Department of Antiquities. It was generously sponsored by Mr. and Mrs. Harry Sacher, Mr. Terence Kennedy and the late Mrs. Kennedy, and the Wolfson Foundation, all of London, and also by the British newspaper, the Sunday *Observer*.

about communications—how to be in touch with the "outside world," how to get your teams to the site, how to bring up the heavy equipment you need for excavating. Also, long before you start digging, you need to have a plan as to where to begin digging, how you propose to go on, how much of the site you intend to cover in the time you have.

So months before October 1963, Yadin and his chief archaeological assistants had gone to the area and made several surveys of the site, some by helicopter. Yadin's first big problem was where to establish his base camp. Here some of his considerations were much the same as those of General Silva in his day.

Should he put it at the foot of the eastern slope and climb and descend each day by the snake path? It would not be as dangerous as it was for Silva's troops, with hostile defenders on the top, but it would be extremely tiring.

On the other hand, an eastern camp would have several advantages. There was a good modern asphalt road leading right to it, via Beersheba and S'dom. Water could be obtained from a nearby youth hostel, whose dining rooms and dormitories could also serve to accommodate the teams.

Or should he put his camp, as Silva had done, near the western side of Masada? The big advantage here was the comparative ease with which one could reach the top. The archaeological teams could use the footpath with the slow gradient that ran alongside the Roman ramp that Silva had built. True, this track did not quite reach the summit, but the gap could be bridged by the construction of a staircase along the steep side of the rock.

A western camp, however, had very grave drawbacks. For one thing, the best site had already been chosen—by the Roman general—and parts of it were still well preserved. No archaeologist would wish to put his headquarters right in the middle of an archaeological site, certainly not one he would be excavating or at least examining.

The chief disadvantage was the absence of a road. Between the asphalt highway near the foot of the snake path and the western slope lay an impassable barrier—the rock of Masada itself! So the highway could not be used; and there was no road across the Judean desert to Masada from the west. The new western one, completed some months earlier, stopped at the newly started desert "town" of Arad, about twenty miles short of Masada. From then on there were only rough tracks, parts covered with huge boulders and parts marked by such uneven ground as large "steps" and hollows, making them impassable to vehicles. Even if they were smoothed, they would be negotiable only by jeeps or trucks with four-wheel drive.

There was the same problem with water and electricity. The pipes and lines served the eastern side of Masada, and those on the west stopped short at Arad. The electricity problem could easily be overcome by installing generators on the site. Water tanks, too, could be set up on the site, but they would need to be filled several times a week by tanker-trucks, and how would these get there with no road?

There was, of course, a third possibility: to establish the camp on the top of Masada! This would have been most convenient. The teams could get up in the morning and within seconds be at their excavations, with no scrambling up the snake path and no trudging over the ramp track. But the objections to this were even stronger than those to "squatting" on Silva's camp. The Masada summit was the main area of the dig, and establishing a base camp there would destroy parts of it and certainly hamper its thorough excavation.

Moreover, the problem of supplies—bringing up food, water, and fuel—would be even greater here than they would for a camp-site at the western foot.

These were some of the "for" and "against" arguments that Yadin and his staff tossed to each other while trying to make up their minds where to pitch their headquarters. Yadin finally decided on the west, choosing a site close to the camp of Roman General Flavius Silva. If the road problem were solved, as well as the problem of a staircase above the ramp path, this camp location would be the most convenient, requiring only a ten-minute gentle climb to the summit. And he knew where to go for help on these problems.

He went to the Israel Army. Like most armies, the Israel Defense Force is deeply interested in tradition. In this case the tradition goes back not just to 1948, when it was established by the newly founded State, but several thousand years —way back to biblical times. Israel army officers are familiar with the military details of most major battles recorded in the Bible. Army courses on the military history of the country, biblical and post-biblical, include an account of the last-stand episode at Masada. Masada, indeed, for obvious reasons, has a special place in the hearts of Israeli army men, and the Tank Corps started a custom a few years ago of conducting a bon-fire oath ceremony for new recruits at the top of Masada, the whole unit climbing up the snake path.

Small wonder, then, that the Army's response to Yadin's request was generous. The staircase would not be easy to construct, but there was no difficulty in securing the Engineers Corps' agreement to undertake it, which they did immediately. The biggest problem was posed by the fact that the ramp path met the west side of Masada at a point several yards below the summit, and this distance was a sheer perpendicular stretch. The staircase had to be built against this rock face and given a solidly constructed base. The engineers were roped and the ropes tied to stakes on the summit. They did most of their work hanging over a chasm. They finished their job quickly, and Masada was accessible by the time the first season of excavation began.

The army engineers also prepared the site of the base camp. Silva had chosen for his site the only level ground in the

Iron staircase at the top of the ramp path built for the expedition by the Israel Army.

western area. To the immediate south of it, where the base camp would now be established, the land was either rocky or "ditchy," deeply cut by dry riverbeds. Army bulldozers smoothed this area, on which would rise three huts to be used as offices of the expedition and a row of tents for the permanent staff on one side of the compound, some fifty tents on the other side for the main body of diggers and other workers, and a dining hall between them. The dining room was a large marquee during the first season and a hut in the second.

Building a western approach road was more complicated, for highway construction was in the hands of the Ministry of Labor, and there were higher priorities on its budget than a road to an archaeological site. The Army agreed to help out by blasting a temporary track for ordinary vehicles but warned that if by some chance there were particularly heavy rains that winter it might not stand up to the traffic. Yadin asked them to build it anyway. They did. Then came the kind of rains that few had remembered experiencing in that region, and there were several stormy days after the excavation had started when even vehicles with four-wheel drive could not get through.

Electricity, as we have said, was provided by generators on the site. As for water, at first it was brought daily by tanker, which filled up the camp's tanks. But when the rains came, the wear and tear on tankers and trucks by the rutted track was so damaging that an alternative had to be found. At one stage, during especially heavy downpours, three days went by before the local tanks were refilled, and the teams were down to a minute ration for drinking. Showers were forbidden during those days.

Then came a discovery by Yadin which he must have welcomed as eagerly as the revelation of some ancient relic. He found an abandoned pipeline. There had been some oil exploration in the area some years before by the NAPHTA oil company, and this length of pipe, running for several miles, had been left.

It was no longer in use. However, it stopped four miles short of Masada.

Yadin called NAPHTA and asked whether he could use it. Yes, they said. He then approached the officers of Mekorot, Israel's national water company, for their urgent assistance. The appeal of Masada was strong, and they readily agreed. After sending down their experts, they cleaned out the old oil pipe and fitted a new, thinner, four-mile-long pipe to its outlet to cover the distance to the camp. The water was fed into the western end of the NAPHTA pipe some twenty miles away, and it reached the Masada camp by gravity flow. After that, the Yadin expedition suffered no water shortage.

With these engineering and "household" problems out of the way or in the process of solution, Yadin then gave thought to personnel. What people would he need? A small group of professional archaeologists, a small group of technicians, and a large body of unskilled but trainable workers to do the heavy and light jobs of excavating, he decided.

The two small groups he already had. The first consisted of archaeologists and advanced students of archaeology. Each would be given a section of the summit and a digging team whose work they would direct and supervise. They would report regularly to Yadin, and they would call him whenever they came across a spectacular find—or if they had an archaeological problem. Also a member of this group, but concerned with the entire area and attached to Yadin, was the architectural expert of the expedition, Dr. Dunayevsky, a man well-experienced in the exploration and study of ancient building.

The second group comprised such technicians as draftsmen, to make drawings of all the finds; the official photographer, to take pictures of the ruins and objects—the objects to be photographed both *in situ*, where they were actually found, and, later, in the studio; a pottery restorer to assemble the broken pieces of pottery and recreate the original vessel; and such other technical personnel as camp commandant, cook, drivers, and so on. The importance of draftsmen, photographer, and pottery restorer is that a study of their work would provide important clues to the archaeologist in the reconstruction of the history of the site. The drawings and photographs would later go into the detailed report of the expedition and the best vessels into a museum, as valuable aids to other scholars.

What of the third group, those engaged in the physical labor of digging? It is customary in most archaeological expeditions anywhere in the world for these to be locally hired laborers. Yadin had used such workers in his previous digs; but with Masada he decided on a completely different course. He had the novel idea of inviting volunteers to join the dig! It is not only that he wished to save money—although all expedition leaders try to do that, however generous their sponsors. He was firmly convinced that the dramatic appeal of the Masada story and the spectacular location of the site would draw a wide response.

There was much to support this conviction. I mentioned earlier the Israeli soldiers' interest in Masada. This deep interest was shared by most of Israel's population, particularly the youth of the country. For many years now, the highlight in the program of most youth movements, pioneer villages (called *kibbutzim*), and scouts and secondary schools is the annual hike to Masada, climbing to the top by the snake path—some even making the trek across the desert as Eleazar did. I have a friend who made the annual climb on his own. Then he got married, and he made the ascent with his wife. Then they had a baby. When the baby was ten months old, the three of them made the climb, the baby straddled on the father's shoulders. They now have four children. All four have reached the top of Masada each year since infancy.

Nor are the young the only ones. There is a man called Yehuda Almog who is well past sixty. He fell in love with the Dead Sea region thirty years ago and has spent most of those years in the area. I often accompanied him on his snake

Two Israel Army volunteers at work on Masada's southeastern casemate wall. A youth hostel and the outlines of the remains of a Roman camp are seen below. In the distance, the Dead Sea.

path climbs to the Masada summit, and he was always ahead of me up the slope.

But perhaps the man who did more than any other to popularize the youth hikes was the remarkable Shmaryahu Guttman, farmer and pioneer *kibbutz* member, who first climbed Masada many years ago and became enchanted by it—enchanted by the region, by the incredible formation of the rock itself, by the fantastic view from its summit, by the drama of the Zealot story, by the mystery of the ruins. He carried out entirely on his own a whole series of explorations, and it was his enthusiasm which sparked the widespread interest of the Israelis in Masada. He was tireless in leading youth hikes to the spot, and from time to time he would take such groups for one or two weeks and camp at Masada. There they would climb where they could, getting to know the site, examining whatever ancient remains were visible.

It was this enthusiasm and interest which Yadin believed would attract numerous Israelis to volunteer.

There was something more—the Israeli passion for archaeology. I know no other country where an archaeological lecture—if the speaker is good—can fill a 3,000-seat auditorium with a non-professional audience several nights running or where even unspectacular discoveries of a dig get such headlines and such detailed coverage in the popular press.

This is partly because Israelis know their Bible in a manner unusual elsewhere. For them it is not only a religious work. It is also a triple textbook—the textbook of their language, Hebrew; their history; and their country's geography. But it is mainly because they live in the land of the Bible and are always aware that the biblical past, which they know so well, lies buried beneath their feet. Scratch the surface in Israel, and you are likely to come across a relic of previous ages. When a child at school reads about David and Goliath, he can visit the site where the duel took place. He can see ruins of cities built by Solomon and picnic in a grove near Samson's birthplace.

Wherever you plough or build, you are likely to hit an important ruin. The best preserved mosaic floor of a sixth century A.D. synagogue was found in the Valley of Jezreel when farmers from the *kibbutz* Beth Alpha went out to dig an irrigation ditch. In Jerusalem recently laborers preparing the foundation for a new house that would have been No. 10 Alfasi Street put their picks through the roof of a cave. They stopped, called the Government Department of Antiquities—which they are required to do by law—and were informed a few days later by the Antiquities' experts that they had uncovered a tomb dating back to the Maccabean period in the second century B.C. The private house never was built. No. 10 Alfasi Street is now the address of a preserved antiquity and open to the public.

With this kind of experience a frequent feature of Israeli life, Yadin had few doubts that many Israeli volunteers would respond.

Then he had another idea. Why confine it to Israelis? Why not open the volunteering to anyone in the world? There might not be many who could be called Masada enthusiasts, but there would be some. There would be quite a number of amateur archaeologists who perhaps had never had the opportunity of joining a professional dig. Some might be attracted by the novelty. Some might think it an offbeat way of spending a holiday. Whatever the reason, study or amusement, scholarship or fun, many, thought Yadin, would wish to come.

He published a brief announcement in the local Israeli press saying that volunteers would be welcomed on the Masada dig. Those accepted would be required to spend at least two weeks with the expedition. Within days, thousands of applications poured in from old and young, individuals and groups, old-time settlers and new immigrants. Among the groups were *Gadna*, a sort of Junior O.T.C. (Officers Training Corps) drawn from high school pupils; *kibbutz* youth; other youth organizations; and units of the Army. Yadin's staff had to wade through the forms and "ration" the applicants. There were more of them than there would be places.

At the same time, a similar announcement appeared in the London Sunday *Observer*, one of the sponsors of the expedition. This also drew thousands of replies. They came from Jews and non-Jews in no less than twenty-eight countries! The Israeli response did not surprise Yadin. But the overseas replies did; for while the purpose was attractive—digging at Masada—the conditions were not. It had been made clear in the announcement that volunteers would have to pay their own fare. This was no free junket. Food and accommodation at Masada would be provided by the expedition; but both would be simple and possibly primitive. The volunteers would sleep under canvas. They would be expected to rise early and put in a full day's work. Although they could dress as they liked and behave as they wished, they would not be permitted to leave Masada without permission—for the site was only a few miles from a hostile border and wandering off alone might be dangerous. Still the applications poured in.

In the end, the expedition was able to run twenty-three two-week shifts of volunteers throughout the two seasons of digging. One group of volunteers would leave on Friday morning, and the next group would be received in the evening. Throughout the entire excavations, the number in the expedition, permanent staff and volunteers, averaged three hundred.

When it was all over, Yadin itemized the professions of the overseas and Israeli volunteers. Here is his list:

Drivers, psychologists, pathologists, students, models, social workers, camera-men (as diggers), priests, vagabonds, geologists, teachers, physiotherapists, pharmacists, miners, editors, professors, shepherds, farmers, actors, architects, artists, librarians, radio-technicians, company directors, contractors, sculptors, housewives, gardeners, waiters, butlers, lawyers, travel agents, factory hands, pilots, accountants, advertisers, doctors, potters, draftsmen, physicists, dentists, tourist guides, bankers, builders, nurses, restorers of antiquities, secretaries, clerks, soldiers, midwives, printers, historians, film directors, violin makers, chambermaids, elephant tamers—and archaeologists.

The final novel course followed at the Masada dig and planned in the preparation stage was for the restoration work to begin simultaneously with the start of the excavation. This is rare in archaeological expeditions. Usually the work of restoration begins—if it is done at all—only after the dig has ended, mainly because the archaeologists rarely know what they will find, and only later can one see which ruins are worth restoring. But at Masada, partly because of Josephus but primarily because of surveys which had been carried out some years before, it was known that there were a few impressive ruins which would be worthy of preservation. After the excavations, several more came to light, and these were restored at the end of the dig.

In general, it may be said that archaeologists on the whole are not normally interested in restoration. They are interested in excavation, digging, cutting away, carefully recording and studying what they find, then cutting away more, recording the finds at the lower level, then continuing to dig away until they reach rock bottom. This enables them to write up what they have found and through this present a three-dimensional picture of the past.

Restoration, on the other hand, is a building up. It means taking an ancient ruin and restoring it so that it looks like the original. It is of interest more to the public than to the scholar, though, of course, the guidance of the archaeologist is necessary if the restoration is to be true and authentic. He will tell the restorer what the original building looked like. He will tell him what system of construction was used at the time. He will point to the stones and pillars lying on the ground and tell him which belong to what building and what goes where.

When the Masada dig was planned, it was decided that such

A section of the archaeologists' camp at the foot of Masada.

a historic and attractive site would be worth restoring, so that the hundreds of thousands of future visitors, who would later be able to reach it easily, could see at a glance what it looked like at the time of the Zealots and could imagine themselves back in the first century. Having the restoration team available during the dig would enable the restorers to receive immediate expert guidance from the archaeologists.

In the particular case of Masada, the restoration team would also be able to give help to the archaeologists. Some of the first century buildings which had survived deliberate destruction had later collapsed. Roofs and walls had fallen in and covered the floors. Under normal conditions, an archaeological expedition would reach the site, see the littered floor, move the collapsed stones to the edge of the summit, probably tip them over the side, and then proceed with the digging. Now, however, they planned that the restoration team would pick up each stone, mark it, and build up the original walls, so that there would be a nice clean floor all ready for the archaeologists to start excavating. Both excavator and restorer would gain.

Yadin received the hearty cooperation of the body responsible for restoration in Israel, the Department for the Preservation of Historic Sites, attached to the Prime Minister's Office. It was headed by Yaacov Yannai. It has now been absorbed by the newly established Israel National Parks Authority, also headed by Yannai. His field man on Masada was Yitzhak Gasco, and he and his team worked for more than two years on the restoration work, remaining on the site during the broiling summer interval between the two digging seasons and continuing long after the expedition had completed its excavations.

The final work of preparation of the men on Yadin's staff was to familiarize themselves with the reports of scholarly visitors to the area in the last century and with the results of Masada studies and surveys in the present century. There had not been many—and none as comprehensive as this would be. Nevertheless, whatever work had been done by earlier scholars had to be studied by this team, just as any archaeologist going out to a site that has been even cursorily explored by others reads every scrap of what they have written.

The first modern explorer to suggest that the particular rock looming over the Dead Sea, which we now know to be Masada, was in fact Masada, was the American scholar, Dr. Edward Robinson. It was then known locally by the name es-Sebbeh. Robinson, accompanied by E. Smith, visited the Dead Sea area in 1838, and they looked at this rock through a telescope. Local Bedouin may have dissuaded them from climbing it, telling them it was very difficult, but they offered the information that on the top were ruins of buildings, some with columns. Through the telescope, wrote Robinson, "I could perceive what appeared to be a building on its northwestern part and also traces of other buildings further east." It was his and his companion's "hunch"—they had little doubt that it was correct—that here was Masada.

Robinson's and Smith's guess was confirmed in March 1842 by another American, a missionary named S. W. Wolcott, who climbed up to and all around the site on a careful inspection tour. He saw the "White Cliff" on the western slope, described by Josephus, and several ruins of buildings on the summit which matched the descriptions in Josephus; and he was the first to come across the Roman camps and their siege wall. It was clear that he was looking at the very features of which he had read in Josephus—the features of Masada.

Other explorers in the nineteenth century who followed Robinson and Wolcott gave additional bits of information, showing without doubt that this was the Masada fortress which Josephus had described. I say "bits of information," for Masada was not the center of their interest. They were exploring the region and had not come to spend all their time on repeated climbs to Masada, which they would have needed to do for a thorough study.

The American Lieutenant W. F. Lynch, of the United States Navy, for example, carried out a survey of the Dead Sea in 1848. Three of his companions, J. B. Dale, H. J. Anderson, and H. Bedlow, rode off from their base on a day's visit to Masada, climbed to the summit, and saw the ruins of several buildings there, one of them located right on the northern point of the rock. They saw "at the distance of about one hundred feet below the northern summit, on an inaccessible precipitous ledge, the remains of a round tower; and forty or fifty feet below that, on another ledge, the foundation walls of a square enclosure. . . ." They added, however, that they "found it impossible to descend to examine these ruins."

There is another description of these ruins, with different figures of distances, in the report of the 1864 climb to the summit by the British prelate, H. B. Tristram. He wrote: "About seventy feet below (fifty as far as we could judge), on a slight projecting ledge, was built up a strong circular fort with double walls and a hollow space of four feet between them. These walls were perfect; but we found it impossible, without ropes, to descend to them. . . . About thirty or forty feet lower still, the rock runs out to a fine point, and on this were the ruins of another fort, quadrangular. . . ." These were in fact not "forts" as Tristram thought, but terraces of a most interesting structure.

In 1867, a British army officer, Captain Warren, was the first in the century to climb the steep eastern face of Masada, and he found parts of the original snake path mentioned by Josephus. He was associated with Kitchener and Conder in their important *Survey of Western Palestine* (published in 1883), undertaken on behalf of the Palestine Exploration

Fund; and it was Lieutenant Conder who described the visible ruins and marked them on the first almost accurate map of the summit of Masada (after a one-day visit in 1875).

There were others. None, however, stayed long at Masada. The first expedition that did was the one led by the German scholar Adolf Schulten, in 1932. They stayed for one month; but their field of interest was the Roman camps and siege works, and they did all their studying around the foot of the rock. Schulten, during those four weeks, visited the summit only twice, spending two mornings sketching the ruins he saw. He must have regretted not being able to excavate, for he wrote: "One can envy the future explorer of the fortress his task, for it is varied and interesting and the magnificent view is a reward in itself."

It is understandable that during the nineteenth and beginning of this century, although explorers did much surveying of the country, none concentrated on Masada. The difficulty of access, the very reason why Herod and later the Zealots chose Masada as their fortress, was also the reason that kept explorers away. To study Masada properly and excavate it meant mounting a large-scale expedition and maintaining it for several months. This required teams of workers, heavy equipment, a lot of money, and a passionate interest. It also required the cooperation and backing of the Government, for many needed services could be provided only by an army, expert and experienced in maintaining units in the field. There was no such government in the country until the establishment of the State of Israel in 1948.

In that year, the Israelis were busy fighting their War of Independence. When the fighting was over, in 1949, Shmaryahu Guttman and the Jewish youth movements resumed their hikes and were more active than ever in focusing interest on Masada. Guttman kept pressing professional archaeologists to undertake a dig, but either there was no money or the likely experts were otherwise engaged. At last, in 1953, his own pioneer *kibbutz* movement backed him to carry out a small survey with the help of enthusiastic *kibbutz* volunteers. They made some important discoveries.

They were the first not only to *see* the "round tower" and "square enclosure," which had been noted by the Lynch team, Tristram, and others but actually reach them. They may have been the first in modern times to do so. Incidentally, Guttman and another pioneer farmer of a *kibbutz*, Micha Livneh, were also probably the first to climb to the top by the precipitous northern edge, exactly where these round and square structures are situated. It was they who correctly identified them for what they are: not parts of fortifications as had been believed, but the remains of a remarkable Herodian building.

It was also this *kibbutz* team, notably one of its prominent members, Azaria Allon, which discovered the ingenious water system that had been installed in Herod's day, complete with cisterns and aqueduct. Guttman is credited with having been the first to trace correctly the original snake path and with the excavation of its gate at the top. He also partially reconstructed one of the Roman camps.

As a result of these discoveries, a more organized expedition of professional archaeologists was undertaken in 1955. It was headed by Professors Michael Avi-Yonah and Nahman Avigad and Dr. (now Professor) Yohanan Aharoni, all of the Hebrew University of Jerusalem; architect Immanuel Dunayevsky and Shmaryahu Guttman. The total group numbered about thirty. In the following year there was a further small expedition of twenty-eight persons, led by Aharoni and Guttman alone. Each of the expeditions lasted only ten days, so that they were more in the nature of limited surveys than full-scale excavations. These archaeologists completed their brief seasons with meager resources and under very difficult conditions, knowing that a thorough dig of the entire site had yet to be made. They said in their report that their "survey included only the remains visible above ground (with two exceptions)";

and after examining the ruins of a building, they would say, for example, that what they had found "leads us to believe that a thorough excavation of this large building would be worthwhile." This was to be done seven years later by the Yadin expedition. But much of what the 1955–56 archaeologists found was important. They established the fact that several of the buildings were definitely built by Herod, and they carried out further exploration of the water system.

Their survey, plus reports of previous surveys and visits, plus the writings of Josephus were what Yadin and his staff had to go on in preparing their excavation plan. There was enough there to whet their appetites, but not enough to disappoint them with the thought that the work had already been done. Indeed, they were convinced that the surface had hardly been scratched. There was almost nothing on the Zealots. As for the Herodian material, it was very useful but a point of departure rather than the last word. The material on the water cisterns was good, yet now they would need to trace the aqueduct and see from where the water was collected. Above all, the reports had dealt with the ruins above ground. No one had yet undertaken any serious digging, and below the ground was where the real treasures of the past lay buried.

In October 1963, as the day the dig was to start dawned, Yadin and his colleagues walked from their base camp along the ramp path to the summit with the feeling that great discoveries were to come. They were about to unlock the secrets of Masada.

3 · THE EXCAVATIONS BEGIN

The volunteers were equally excited as they made their way to the summit along the same path on the opening day of the dig.

It was Sunday, but since the Jewish Sabbath is Saturday, Sunday is the start of Israel's work week. Those from overseas had arrived in Israel a few days earlier, some by plane, some by ship, with instructions to assemble in the municipal gardens of Beersheba at midday on Friday. For those who knew their Bible, the very name Beersheba was touched with romance. Situated in the Negev, Israel's southern desert, Beersheba was the meeting place for the patriarch Abraham and Abimelech, king of Gerar.

In Beersheba the overseas volunteers were received by a member of the expedition staff. Together with the Israeli volunteers they numbered some two hundred. The permanent staff, laborers, and volunteers from the Army were not with them. After lunching, their baggage was put aboard trucks and sent on to the base camp via Arad to reach Masada by the rough-tracked western approach. The volunteers themselves were taken by bus along another route. They drove smoothly along a modern highway straight to S'dom, the ill-fated twin city of Gomorrah of the Bible, at the southern tip of the Dead Sea. It is today the site of a modern potash plant, and it does not look at all ill-fated. The drive lasted an hour along gentle curves and slow gradients, which in the final twenty minutes brought them down from 1,200 feet above to 1,200 feet below sea level.

They then proceeded northward along the narrow western shore of the Dead Sea, the edge of the Judean desert on their left, the water on their right. After about half an hour, they turned off the road onto a track leading inland toward the hills. They bumped their way for a few hundred yards, and the buses stopped. They got off. Looming in front of them was the rock of Masada. They were almost at the foot of its eastern slope.

Their guide pointed to the top of Masada and said, "That's our target." When he saw the questioning look in their eyes, he drew their attention to a thin ribbon of white that zig-zagged its way up the gray and reddish stony slope. They were about to make the ascent by the snake path. Josephus was right. It looked very much like a long serpent, twisting and winding across the rock face.

Their guide reassured them. "You'll only have to do this once," he said. "But don't worry. It's not so tough as it looks. We'll take it gently, and we'll be at the top in an hour. To get the feel of Masada, you should be conscious of its height, and the most impressive way to do this is to climb the snake path. From tomorrow on, you'll be getting to the summit from the other side, the western side, and that's easy. I should add that even the snake path is easier today than it used to be before the Army made it passable and safe. They also built up and added stairs to the bit near the top where it had col-lapsed or was worn away.

"One thing more," he went on. "Please tread firmly and try

Aerial view of northern section of Masada summit showing the upper part of the snake path meeting the casemate wall to the left of the remains of Herod's storerooms.

not to dislodge any stones, as they may fall on the people below you on the slope."

They started. The pace was slow and steady, and the ascent did not seem at all difficult, certainly not for the younger ones in the party. It was rather fun. They would move along one "leg" of the zigzag in one direction, and then the path would almost turn back on itself at a hairpin angle and move off and slightly up in the other direction. Think of the path, if you like, as the track of skiers doing long left and right traverses across the slope, with sharp angles at the turns. (Except that the volunteers were going up, not down, and it was very much hotter than is usual on a ski run.)

The higher they went, the better the view. The water of the Dead Sea at this time of day was a full blue, and far beyond the eastern shore were the mountains of Moab, now a flaming red. Toward evening, they would turn to purple in the waning sun. None of the rocks at the edge of the Judean escarpment to the north and south was as impressive as the rock of Masada, although many had strange shapes, twisted into these forms by that great prehistoric event which had split the earth between the territories now known as Turkey and Africa, and since eroded by time. The Dead Sea itself, lying so low, is one result of that split. Some of these rocks were reminiscent of early science-fiction pictures of the landscape of the moon.

As they climbed, those volunteers who had read Josephus were delighted to find that he had grossly exaggerated the terrors of the snake path. It was nothing like "balancing on a tightrope." As for his "on either side yawns an abyss so terrifying that it could make the boldest tremble"—there was an abyss only on one side, and it was not really an abyss, just a steep slope. Josephus had also written that "the least slip means death." It is true that a few Israeli youths had been killed; but that had been in earlier years, before the Army had widened and repaired the path and added supporting platforms near the turns. It may well have been more dangerous in Josephus' time but hardly so terrifying as he claimed.

About halfway up, the older ones began to puff, and there were more frequent rests. That is why it took about an hour and a quarter before the last of the group reached the top.

There was a feeling of general excitement when the volunteers took their first steps on the summit. The guide had been right. They did have a deeper sense of the isolation of Masada, high and gaunt and remote, dominating the surroundings. Climbing it from the east had also given them a sense of achievement.

To top off this feeling, they were offered a view of enchanting beauty. They could see for miles and miles in all directions—to Moab in the east; the Araba valley to the south, stretching away toward the Red Sea; and to the west and the north, the Judean desert. It was a scene of ruggedness and color and timelessness. They were looking at the same sights that had greeted the eyes of those who had stood on this summit nineteen hundred years earlier—and whose secrets they were about to dig up.

It was a fine prelude to an archaeological excavation.

They were happy, but they were also tired and hungry. Their guide led them across the top of Masada to the western edge, where they went down the newly installed and steep staircase. This put them on the path that skirted the Roman ramp, and, of course, gave them their first glimpse of the ramp. It looked massive and solid—as it must have been to have lasted so many centuries; and how amazing that it had taken only a few months to build, and under such trying conditions. One forgot, for the moment, that thousands of slaves had labored on it.

They were also within sight of their base camp, a tented compound, and within minutes they were there. They were quickly "processed"—told to which group they were assigned, given the number of their tent, and provided with ration

Helicopter view of the Roman ramp and the ramp path.

Volunteers descending the path alongside the ramp. The head of the cable rail installed for the excavations can be seen top right.

tickets for their fortnight of meals. The digging would be carried out by six groups, each headed by a professional archaeologist, each responsible for excavating one section of the summit.

With sleeping accommodation arranged—eight to a tent—they went off to collect their baggage and then proceeded to the showers. These were primitive, but there was hot water, and it was good to get rid of the snake path dirt. Refreshed, they went to the dining hut for an early supper. After eating, they were shown a documentary film of Masada and then given a short talk on the administrative arrangements. On work days, they would rise at dawn and be at their labors by five thirty. A sandwich lunch would be brought to them on the summit and they would work until three in the afternoon. Thereafter they would be free. For evening entertainment there would be a feature film once or twice a week, a concert, folk singers, and popular artistes brought from Tel-Aviv. The archaeological staff would have a nightly meeting to review the discoveries of the day.

The first night was romantic, and most of them sat out under the sky. Although it was October, the air was soft and warmish, and the blackness lifted as the moon came up over Masada, a three-quarter moon of a brightness unknown in the countries of the west. The stars, too, seemed unusually luminous, abundant, and close. Few of the visitors had known that these were the typical features of an "eastern sky," especially over the desert.

It was with reluctance that many of the volunteers dragged themselves away and into their camp beds. They were warned that they would be up early next morning—not as early as on a digging day but still early for a Sabbath—to start a five-hour tour of the excavation site.

At eight thirty the next day, washed and breakfasted, and after a ten-minute walk up the ramp path, they were all on the summit awaiting their introduction to Masada. They were divided into two groups, one Hebrew-speaking, the other to be addressed in English, each under the charge of one of Yadin's archaeological assistants who would be giving the "briefing"— an account of the history of the site, an explanation of the visible ruins, and an outline of the excavation program—where they would dig, what they hoped to find, and some preliminary instructions on how the volunteers would go about their archaeological work.

The overseas group were led off to the northern section of the summit, and there they ranged themselves in a semicircle on a heap of large boulders and listened to their archaeologist-guide.

First he told them the story of the site, all about Herod and later the Zealots and the Roman assault and its startling end. He frequently broke off his account to read aloud the relevant passages in Josephus. Some of his listeners knew their Josephus, but reading it at home was vastly different from hearing the words right on Masada itself. As he read, the instructor would point to the ruin, if it were visible, or to the location referred to by Josephus. They could see the ramp the Romans had built. They could see the outline of Silva's camp, just as the Zealots had in their day, and were struck by its closeness. They could see the point where the battering ram would have reached the casement wall—although they could not see the wall because the place where it was presumed to be was covered with rubble. They could see parts of the circumvallation. Conscious that they were on the very spot where the Zealots had stood, and listening to the ancient words, the volunteers were sped on a journey in time, back through nineteen centuries. They were reliving the first century story.

This is how each group of Masada volunteers began their archaeological fortnight. The briefing over, they would be led on a well-guided tour of the summit. At the northernmost point they saw the ruins of a most remarkable building. This was the one containing the round and square structures that had been spotted by the nineteenth century explorers.

Those who had been assigned to the team that would be excavating here took special notice of what they saw. The rest did the same when they came to inspect the sections that they would be digging. All were greatly taken by this spectacular northern building. It had been built in three layers, or tiers, or terraces, on the very point of the rock, the middle terrace extending beyond the top level and the lowest terrace extending beyond the middle one. To anyone viewing it in profile from a distance, either from the west or the east, it looked like three gigantic steps cut at the top of the cliff side. From where the volunteers stood, on the summit, level with the upper terrace, it was like standing on the bridge of a huge ship viewing two decks below, the lowest jutting out beyond the other. The round structure was on the middle terrace, the square "enclosure" on the bottom one. Both were partly covered by rubble.

Internal staircases had originally connected the three tiers, but these were not now visible. What now linked the three terraces was a series of newly installed iron steps clinging to the side of the rock. They had been built by the army engineers especially for the expedition and for later visitors to the site. The work had been difficult and hazardous. The sappers used hanging scaffolds staked to the summit, and all were roped as they labored above the precipice. Safety was supervised by an expert on cables, ropes, and knots who had been called in from the Israel Navy.

If it was tough and dangerous for the modern Army to install an improvised staircase, what must it have been like in the first century B.C. for the engineers engaged on the permanent structure!

The volunteers were introduced briefly to the conflicting views of archaeologists as to what Herod had intended this

View of the hanging palace, or palace-villa, from the west.

building to be. It seemed to match most, although not all, of the description of Herod's "palace" that appears in Josephus, an identification supported by the 1955–56 expedition. But Schulten had ascribed the palace to another building on the western section of the summit. One of the jobs of the expedition would be to clear up this problem.

Even more important would be to discover ancient remains among the debris or hidden beneath a floor or behind a wall. Whatever this building turned out to be, it must have been something special. Such remarkable architecture and such daring engineering would not have been employed for anything ordinary. If it was special when Herod built it, it must have remained special in the time of the Zealots. If the Zealots had wished to save any possessions from falling into Roman hands, and if for some reason such possessions could not be destroyed, the hiding place might well have been chosen in this building. And the possessions that they would have hidden rather than destroyed would, most naturally, have been sacred writings. It was Yadin's theory that the devout Zealots would have brought their holy books with them to Masada, and when the end came, not wishing them to be taken and despoiled by the Romans, they would have put them in some secret place; for the Zealots would have been strict followers of the Jewish rule that sacred Hebrew writing must not be destroyed. To this day, religious Jews do not destroy old Hebrew prayer books. When, after constant synagogue use, they become tattered and torn, they are buried in the sacred, or what is called consecrated, ground of a cemetery.

It was thus likely that holy scrolls would have been hidden, and if so, there was a reasonable chance that the expedition would find them. A discovery of scrolls would make the whole venture worthwhile, and the volunteers were instructed to be particularly careful in excavating this section and on the lookout for fragments of parchment.

Some of them may well have thought that the finding of

scrolls would be largely a matter of luck. Actually, in archaeology, as in other branches of scholarship, knowledge and reasoning count for more than luck. Of course, there is the element of luck in all discovery, even in areas where the need for technical knowledge is great. In archaeology, though, with its flavor of the treasure hunt, people tend to put more emphasis on the role of chance. An archaeologist who finds nothing is called unlucky; one who makes a great discovery is called lucky. But it is not as simple as that. Good results in an archaeological expedition will often be found to have been the result of wide reading, deep knowledge, a good memory of what was discovered at other archaeological excavations, imaginative reasoning, and keen judgment. In these respects, a good archaeologist is like a good detective or a good army intelligence officer. He must know what clues to look for, be able to recognize them when he finds them, and then judge, often by a flash of intuition, the meaning to which they point.

An archaeologist with little knowledge will waste a lot of time and at the end find little if he goes to a site and starts digging at random. Even if he goes to a site like Masada, where some ancient ruins are already visible above the surface, he will miss much unless he can make a sound appreciation in advance of where the most important remains are likely to be. The leader of an expedition has comparatively little time and manpower. He cannot turn up every cubic inch of soil. He must make a choice. Where will he dig? How much time—and how many diggers—will he assign to each section? This is always a difficult problem. It is decided not by chance, not by tossing a coin, but by careful thought. Otherwise the leader may find himself spending months on a section that yields little and allocating only a few days to one that might have offered much. This is not to say that such useful advance thinking is always possible with a virgin archaeological site. But it was with Masada. What Yadin did, therefore, assuming the historical record in Josephus was true, was to put himself first in the shoes of Herod and then in the position of the Zealots. "If I were Herod," he virtually said to himself, knowing Herod's character and the political background of the times in which Herod lived, "and was fortifying Masada, what structures would I need, and where would I place them? What would I do for food and water?" The same with Eleazar ben Ya'ir. How would he live on the summit with his Zealot group? How would he react to Roman siege and assault? What would Eleazar have done, apart from what Josephus had described, before the final deed was committed?

The good detective does the same; he puts himself in the shoes of the criminal he is chasing, trying to work out the moves he would make; and the army commander also tries to read the mind of the enemy, to imagine what his next step will be so that he can meet it. The archaeologist is not after an enemy or a criminal, but after relics of the past, and he, too, tries to conjure up the thinking of the people whose remains he seeks.

Luck enters the picture in the quality of the finds. Wisdom and intuition and reasoning may lead an archaeologist to the ancient remains; but when he gets to them, he may see that they were not worth finding. They may have disintegrated with time, or, if they are in good condition, they may add little of value to existing archaeological knowledge. Then one might say that the archaeologist is unlucky; and if the discoveries are in good condition and important, that he is lucky.

There were several occasions during the period the expedition was at Masada when it could be said to have been "lucky" in that sense—the finds were important and in a good state of preservation; but the archaeologists were led to them by foresight and logical reasoning.

The groups were next taken to the ruins of a cluster of buildings immediately south of the northern three-tiered structure. These were the ones that earlier scholars had determined were the storerooms built by Herod. They were covered by debris, and strewn over the site were many large oblong stones, clearly cut by man, which must have fallen when the walls collapsed. Some of these buildings would be cleared and the walls restored by a special restoration team before excavation work would start here.

Visible to the west of the storehouses were parts of the ruin of what must have been a large building, most of it buried beneath mounds of debris. No one had quite worked out what it could have been, although there were several theories. Most suggested that it must have had some connection with the storehouses: perhaps an office to administer the supply and distribution of the stores; perhaps a tower to guard them. The archaeologists were keeping an open mind on the subject and hoped that excavation would give them the answer. The answer was to prove startling and the discovery one of the most attractive spots on Masada today.

Next, walking to the south, the volunteers came across the ruins of a large square building. This was what Schulten had called the "small palace" and what the 1955–56 expedition had thought might have served the royal garrison in the time of Herod and the Roman garrison that occupied Masada later. Here, too, the expedition was to find a more accurate answer after excavation—and as a bonus to discover some precious articles hidden beneath the original floor of one of the rooms.

A few yards to the southwest of this building were the well-preserved walls and floor of an easily identifiable structure—a church. This, in fact, had for long been the most conspicuous ruin on the summit, and early visitors in the nineteenth century had already established that this was a Christian sanctuary built during the Byzantine period, in the fifth or sixth century A.D. Yadin's excavation plans did not call for a good deal of work on this site. For one thing, it was doubtful whether anything of great significance would be found after the study, even though it was brief, of this building by a certain scholar named F. de Saulcy in the middle of the last century. Yadin's main reason, however, was that his primary interest lay in the Herodian and Zealotian periods and this Byzantine structure was "too new." However, some excavation would be carried out, if only for the sake of completeness, for de Saulcy had done no major digging and had largely concerned himself with what was visible above the surface.

What the expedition *would* be spending time on was the ruins of a huge building to the southwest of the church. This was what Schulten had identified as *the* palace of Herod as described by Josephus and the 1955–56 expedition had thought was *a* palace but not the one Josephus had had in mind. It was clearly a building of great importance, which would be worth excavating thoroughly.

The only other visible ruins on the summit to which the volunteers were taken on their introductory tour were two small clusters to the southeast of "Schulten's palace." These would be subjected to a routine dig. There were other parts of the summit that contained no visible remains but would also be excavated. Who knew? Perhaps it would be precisely there that the chief discoveries would be made.

The tour was completed with a walk around the perimeter of Masada where Josephus said Herod had built a casemate wall studded by a series of towers. But the group saw nothing that looked like a wall, just rows of stone piles along some sections. However, during the earlier preparations by the expedition staff, air photographs had been taken of the entire site, and these revealed the outlines of the foundations of a double wall. Some members of the staff had also carried out a quick sample study on the ground of a few sections that had shown up sharply on the photographs, and their conclusions were very hopeful. On the basis of these results and the photographs, it had been decided to assign a large number of expedition members to working on this casemate wall. It proved a wise decision. Something like half the total volunteer groups found themselves clearing and digging the wall throughout the entire eleven months of the two seasons of excavations. Most of what we know today of the Zealots is based on the finds in the casemate wall.

Each fortnightly "shift" of volunteers, their archaeological appetites whetted by the Saturday morning tour, would start their digging sessions shortly after dawn the following day.

They were always a gay sight as they climbed the ramp path to Masada's summit. They were dressed in "working clothes" which they had been asked to bring from home, but there was nothing uniform about them. The variety of styles and colors was unbelievably wide. There were girls in sandals, slacks, and jumpers; some in shorts and blouses; some in hard-wearing skirts and jackets. One girl, when the sun moved almost overhead toward midday, shed her slacks and worked in a bikini. The men wore mostly shorts and shirts—removing the shirts as it grew hotter. Only some of the Israeli old-timers, not caring about acquiring a fashionable tan, followed the clothing practice of this part of the world and exposed as little as possible to the burning sun.

Arriving at the top, each of the six working groups was led by the archaeologist supervisor to its section of the site. Professor Yadin was with them, but he spent the day moving from one to another, guiding, directing, explaining, consulting with the section supervisors on each stage of the dig.

The area supervisors always explained to the volunteers on their first day what they would be doing and how. It would be their job to dig down through the various levels of human settlement in their particular area of Masada, carefully examining all the earth and debris for ancient remains. What they found, and the record of where and at what depth, would then be assessed by the professional archaeologist to provide a physical history of the site.

What is meant by "levels of human settlement?" Think of a

piece of ground in the distant past that has never been occupied by human beings. Then along come people who decide to settle on it, establishing a town or a village or a fortress. They build, they live there, they farm, they fight, they trade, they cook. After a time—it may be ten years, fifty years, one hundred years—they are attacked by a strong enemy, and their settlement is destroyed. Or there is an earthquake, and their village collapses. Or there is a fire, and everything gets burned. Or the villagers, perhaps threatened by a powerful foe, just get up and leave, abandoning their homes.

Sometime later, other people come along and build a new village or town or fortress on the earlier ruins—for even the buildings of an abandoned settlement eventually collapse. This second settlement, in its time, suffers the fate of the first. Later, there may be a third settlement, built on the ruins of the second. And so it goes on. In some places, like Megiddo in Israel— the site of the legendary Armageddon—archaeologists found that there had been no less than twenty cities, built one on top of the other, during the 3,000 years or so between 3,500 B.C. and 300 B.C.

The remains of the very first settlement would of course be contained in the very lowest level, or layer, or, as the archaeologists call it, *stratum—strata* in the plural. This would be the level closest to rock bottom. Among those remains, depending on how old the settlement was, the archaeologist might find ruins of buildings; tools; jars, plates, and other vessels of pottery, either whole or broken; dried remains of food; bones of humans and animals; coins (at a later period); writing (also at a later period); idols; drawings, sculpture, and other works of art; cooking pots; olive presses; and so on. By examining these finds—the plan of a building, the way a stone wall was built, the shape of a vessel, the way the pottery was made, the tools that were used, the form of an arrowhead—the experienced archaeologist can tell how, and the period when, these people lived. If they lived up to about 4,000 years ago, the archaeologist—in Israel, at least, because of the considerable work done in Biblical archaeology—can give their date to the nearest century. If it was as recent as 2,000 years ago, he might come closer and place it to the nearest fifty years.

The second settlement would leave a similar layer or stratum of remains. So would the third and subsequent settlements. When the archaeologist begins his work, therefore, the stratum he comes across first, the one nearest the surface, is the newest and youngest. The deeper he digs, the more ancient the settlement. Thus, on Masada, one could expect to encounter remains of the Zealots before the remains of Herod.

This explains the importance of recording not only the area where an object is found but also the stratum in which it is embedded. Unfortunately, an archaeological site is not like a fancy cake where every layer is sharply defined and easy to detect. There is no rigid line, no handy sign saying, "You are approaching Stratum 3 belonging to the eighteenth century B.C." To the layman all might look the same, and he could dig his way from Stratum 10 to Stratum 2 without discerning any layers and without knowing that he may have gone from A.D. 500 to 500 B.C.

The professional archaeologist will determine a stratum only after examining its remains. This is not always easy. There are many pitfalls. An archaeologist will see a vessel whose shape, texture, and design show it to belong to the fourth century A.D., and if he is inexperienced, he may automatically think that the stratum in which it was found is fourth century. But the stratum may be later, perhaps fifth century A.D., and someone in that later period may have found this old vessel and preserved it. Or, which is more common, people building on the ruins of an earlier city may use the stones and columns of these ruins as building material for their new structures. Again, the inexperienced scholar may tend to date the stratum of this new settlement by the date of the stones and columns of the older settlement. The good professional always looks for confirming clues before he commits himself to defining and dating an archaeological level.

The Masada site was marked off into several excavation areas and each area given a number. The areas were subdivided into sections, and these were numbered, too. So were the different levels as the digging proceeded. Every find could thus be registered with the numbers of the location and stratum where it was discovered.

Each group of volunteers assigned to an area was split up into sub-groups of four to six persons and each sub-group assigned a section to excavate.

The area supervisor introduced the volunteers to their working tools. Kept permanently on their site were large picks to attack stubborn stone and rock; small handpicks to loosen earth or debris; small hoes to remove it; whisk brushes and a broom to clear each excavated surface; rubber pails to receive the debris; a large sieve to sift it; a wheelbarrow into which the sifted debris would fall and be carted away; plastic buckets to receive the bits of broken pottery; and small cardboard boxes for small objects that might be found, such as arrowheads, coins, and other metal articles, and items of glass, wood, or bone. There were also tags marked with the number of the area and subdivision, which would be attached to the plastic buckets and boxes containing the finds. In addition, the supervisor had a plumb line and spirit level to insure that the sides and floor of the excavation were straight and true. He was also in charge of the large-scale plan of his area on which he would mark progress and the location of the finds.

The first task in each section was clearance of the large boulders. Then the stones. Then the mounds of earth and debris. It was left to the sub-group to decide on the functions of each individual—who did what. There was gallantry in most teams: the heavier task of removing boulders and stones was done by the men, although all would lend a hand while

Diggers removing boulders to clear a section of the Byzantine chapel.

waiting to get at the debris. The lighter job of gathering this into the rubber buckets was done for the most part by the women, although when the men were not busy on something heavier, they too would handpick and hoe and scrape, which was the real and most interesting job of excavation.

The next job was examining the debris. When a bucket was full, it was carried to the wheelbarrow and tipped onto the sieve that lay on the barrow. Two persons, usually the one in charge of the barrow and the one who had brought the bucket, would shake the oblong sieve. Whatever remained on top was kept—pottery in the plastic pails, other items in the boxes. The debris in the barrow was then wheeled away to a temporary dumping site, later to be tipped over the side of Masada by bulldozer.

With the heavier work of stone clearance completed, the teams usually found they worked best with two of their members scraping away the earth and debris; two carrying the buckets to the sieve and sifting and tying tags to the containers of finds; and one on the barrow, helping with the sieve and then removing the sifted debris. During the day, they would switch jobs.

The area supervisor was with his group all the time, going from one section to another to follow their progress. His first act, with each visit, was to examine the cardboard boxes to see what new objects had been found.

When they were particularly important, he would call Yadin to inspect them. When they were of startling importance, like a scroll or a cache of coins, the excitement in the section was so contagious that within minutes almost the entire expedition would come crowding over to see.

It was easy to explain the "contagion." Yadin would be seen rushing to the spot, followed by a hurrying photographer

A volunteer from the United States helps sift debris.

—the official expedition photographer—and it would be evident to all that "something was up." For the volunteers had been given strict instructions that when they came across something that appeared to be of unusual importance, they were to stop digging and immediately call their supervisor. They might be scraping a wall or excavating a floor and find the edge of something sticking out—an unbroken glass vessel, part of a skeleton, a pouch of documents. If the supervisor confirmed that it was important, they would wait until Yadin had made his inspection, and then the photographer would film the object in the position in which it was found. The supervisor himself would then complete the careful scraping around the object until it could be removed.

The general run of small objects would remain in their boxes on the site and be taken to the expedition office below when work was over for the day. The buckets of broken pottery, however, were sent down immediately by conveyor cable, which the Army had installed. They reached a special washing area near the camp where other volunteers washed and cleaned them and deposited them in another container also marked with the number of the area-subdivision-layer in which they were found.

Why such careful handling of broken pottery—a practice which is observed now at all archaeological excavations?

We have already seen that it is of the highest importance for an archaeologist to be able to date each stratum he excavates and to do so as accurately as possible. Pottery is one of the major keys to archaeological dating. By examining a piece of pottery, the experienced scholar can tell at what period in history it was made. If there are many similar vessels, or pieces of such vessels, in a particular stratum, he can usually conclude that the stratum belongs to that period. The archaeological term for bits of broken pottery is *potsherds*, often called *sherds* or *shards*.

Why should sherds be so useful a clue to chronology?

In this part of the world, the art of making pots, at first by hand and later on the potter's wheel, became general in the Bronze Age (3,150 B.C. to 1,200 B.C.). With its common use, pottery was plentiful. Since it broke easily, it was frequently replaced. Such replacement offered the potters more frequent opportunities to make improvements, introducing changes—more so, for example, than with metal vessels. Thus, each succeeding period could be identified by the special shape and design of the pottery developed in it.

Moreover, since the broken pieces were valueless, they remained on the site where their owners lived. In time of emergency, if these owners abandoned their town or village, they might carry with them precious vessels of silver and gold or precious items of ivory. But not the potsherds. If they were conquered, the victors might remove precious objects as loot but not sherds. When, some time later, another group of settlers occupied the site and found remains of the earlier occupants, they might use some items like stone columns for building materials or perhaps an olive press or undamaged vessels, but they would ignore the broken pottery.

Thousands of years later, as archaeologists began to dig up the past, they would thus find huge quantities of these sherds littered about the different strata. For though pottery might break easily, the pieces were almost indestructible. Since the sherds were valueless at the time they were broken and would not therefore have been removed, it could be presumed that they belonged to the same period as the stratum in which they were discovered.

All this seems very logical to us today. In fact the idea of potsherds serving as clues to dates occurred only in the 1880's, when it flashed into the brilliant mind of the British archaeologist, Sir Flinders Petrie. Before then, archaeologists were mostly interested in complete objects—statues, tablets with inscriptions, unbroken pottery vessels. "Useless" sherds were usually left behind, together with other valueless debris.

In 1884–85 Petrie was excavating in Egypt, and he came across the remains of an ancient settlement, among which were broken pieces of vases that looked familiar to him. They were similar to Greek-style painted vases that had been discovered in Etruscan tombs during the eighteenth and nineteenth centuries. (The Etruscans, so called because they were natives of Etruria, were a people who lived in north central Italy from about the eighth century B.C. onwards. They are believed to have come from the Greek parts of Asia Minor. Their pottery, from the eighth to the third centuries B.C., followed the ceramic styles of Greece.)

Now, these Etruscan vases, because they were valuable as objects of art, had been carefully studied, and scholars had finally determined their dates. Petrie compared the sherds he found in Egypt with them and saw that they were similar to the Etruscan objects which belonged to the sixth century B.C. This helped him date the Egyptian settlement he had excavated. It turned out to be a Greek colony, the long-lost city of Naukratis.

Seven years later, Petrie was excavating a site in Israel (Palestine at the time), and remembering his pottery experience, paid careful attention to the sherds he came across at each level. He found the remains of several superimposed cities, *and each had its characteristic pottery!* From then on, pottery became an important subject of study for every archaeologist and the examination of sherds an essential job at any excavation. So did other innovations introduced by Petrie, followed by all who came after him, including the expedition at Masada: the careful examination and recording of every item, however valueless it seemed and however fragmentary, and the recording, too, in what position of the level it was found.

After every excavation, the final scholarly report—which is often boring to the layman but of intense interest to other archaeologists—will contain pages and pages of drawings of vessels reconstructed from potsherds found at each level. There will be several drawings of each vessel, showing how it looks from different angles, with details of any ornamentation, the materials used, the technique of manufacture. Students of archaeology equip themselves with this knowledge, so that when they come to excavate a new site, they are familiar with the shape and design of vessels belonging to each century of settlement in the region.

At Masada, the range of sherds was more limited than is usual in this country, for it was unlikely, if Josephus was right, that remains would be found of much human habitation earlier than the second century B.C. and later than the Byzantine church, fifth or sixth century A.D. Still, the standard modern archaeological practice was followed and careful attention paid to the potsherds. These, as we have said, were sent down to the washing sheds all the time. Later, often after the excavation season was over, they would be examined with great care by the professional archaeologists. It was a less adventurous but equally important part of the archaeologist's life, although some scholars regard the examination of the finds and the deductions they make from them as exciting as the digging. This also was the difference between the professionals and the volunteers.

The volunteer sherd washers were told to keep an eye out for two things. Their first and most important task was to look for any writing or inscription or marking on the pieces of pottery. An inscription was often invisible until the sherd was cleaned. If, after washing, it was found to bear some kind of marking, it was put in a box and marked with the site and stratum number and shown to Yadin as soon as he came down from the summit. In ancient days, even after parchment and paper came into use, bits of pottery would be used for such things as receipts or chits or labels, or they may have been parts of a vessel with a longer inscription. At Masada, one of the most dramatic finds would be eleven such sherds, each bearing a name, which was to prove of immense interest. Incidentally, a sherd with writing on it is called an *ostracon—ostraca* in the plural.

The second thing they were to look out for in washing the pottery was whether several bits seemed to belong to the same vessel. There were other members of the expedition whose job was pottery reconstruction, as far as this was possible. The volunteers who did best at this were those who were good at jigsaw puzzles, though it was surprising how many who were trying it for the first time soon became adepts. At the beginning of the day one might see them beside a pile of potsherds, and by the afternoon the sherds would have become a beautiful jar or vase or bowl.

This was fun; but the amateur archaeologists who were scraping away at the top often got bored with the pottery sherds. It was fine the first day, when anything one found was exciting, even a bit of an old mug. After a while, however, since there were so many of them, to the non-professionals, who would neither be assembling them nor studying them later, they were just what they were—pieces of broken crockery. Besides, even those who were not lucky enough to make an outstanding find, like a scroll or a hoard of coins or the ruins of an unexpected building, soon found "ordinary" things other than sherds to capture their interest. Removing the rubble and finding the floor of a room was exciting. So was finding the foundation stones of a building, part of a wall, charred fragments showing that there had been a fire. These were "routine" finds, which most of the volunteers experienced throughout both seasons of the dig. It fell to only a few sub-groups in each batch of volunteers to witness a spectacular discovery—"new" ruins of magnificent structures, mosaic floors, wall decorations, scroll fragments, ostraca, rare coins,

A volunteer from England reconstructing an ancient pot.

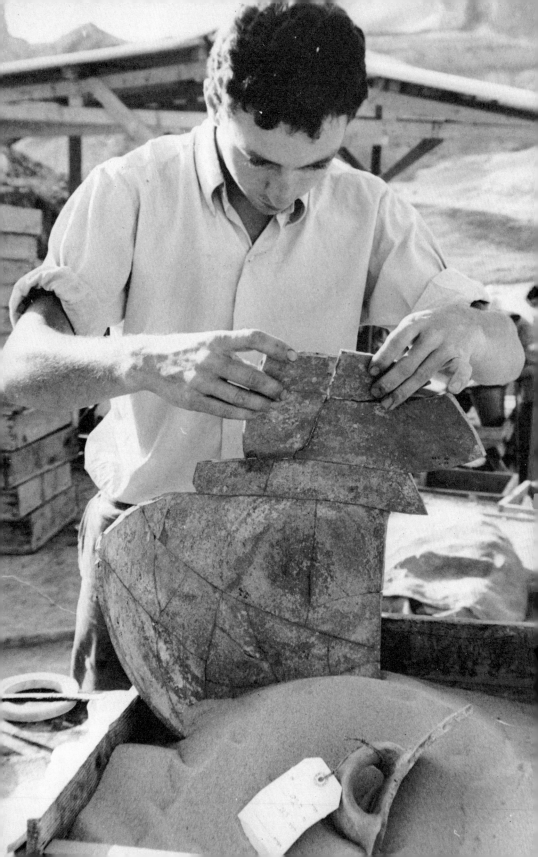

ammunition balls, scales of armor, arrowheads, remnants of food, complete stone vessels, unbroken pottery jars, cooking stoves, and lots of other things, including such cosmetic items as a wooden comb and a box of eye paint (!), interesting in themselves to the lay volunteer and of importance to the archaeologist.

PART II · THE DISCOVERIES

Aerial view of Masada taken from the northwest.

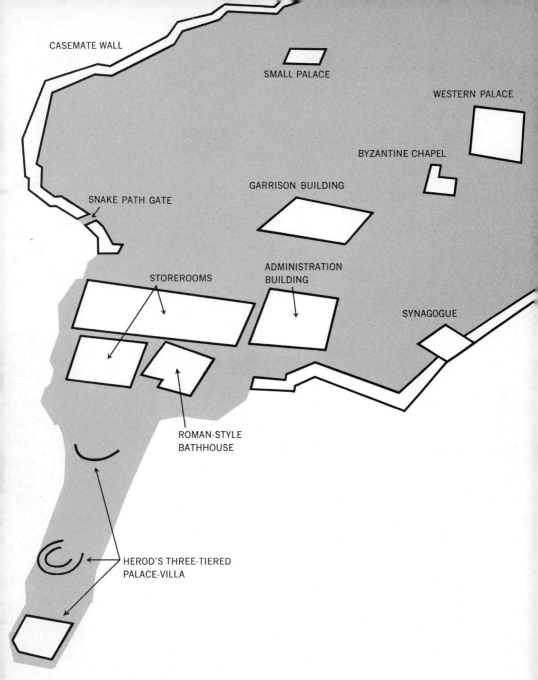

CASEMATE WALL

SMALL PALACE

WESTERN PALACE

BYZANTINE CHAPEL

GARRISON BUILDING

SNAKE PATH GATE

ADMINISTRATION
BUILDING

STOREROOMS

SYNAGOGUE

ROMAN-STYLE
BATHHOUSE

HEROD'S THREE-TIERED
PALACE-VILLA

Diagram based on the view of Masada at left.

4 · THE BUILDINGS OF HEROD

The Water System

Historians had long wondered how Herod, and later the Zealots, had solved the water problem, for the region is notoriously short of water. There is no spring in the vicinity and very little rainfall. How, then, could some thousand Zealots have lived there for several years? If they had brought water from some distant source, what had they done in the final months when they were under siege and never left the site?

Josephus wrote that there were water cisterns cut in the rock of Masada and that these insured a plentiful supply. Cisterns cut into the summit had been seen and examined by all who had climbed to the top. They were served by no visible source and were obviously fed by waters from elsewhere. But from where?

In 1953, the Guttman *kibbutz* team decided to investigate something they had seen on their frequent visits. If you stand near Silva's camp and face Masada, to the left of the ramp, about halfway up the northwestern slope, you see a series of what look like holes in the rock—or rather two series, one above the other. No one had ever climbed up to take a close look and find out for certain what they were. These *kibbutznicks* did.

They found that the "holes" were openings in the rock, leading to huge man-cut caverns. These were in fact the water cisterns Josephus certainly had in mind. And as early as the nineteenth century, Lynch's assistants had ventured the thought that they were possibly reservoirs. Walls, floor, and ceiling of each cistern were lined with a smooth, white, water-resistant plaster. Near the entrance to each opening were steps cut in the rock that led down to the floor. Some of the cisterns were full of debris.

As they moved along the face of the Masada slope, Guttman's group noticed traces of an ancient aqueduct, a manmade water channel, near the mouth of each cistern. There was further evidence that this part of the aqueduct led to another part in the valley separating the rock of Masada from the main plateau of the Judean desert.

These explorations were continued by the 1955–56 expedition, and the bulk of what is known today about the cisterns and the water system as a whole—which was the work of Herod's engineers—is due to these earlier studies, although it fell to the Yadin expedition to discover the precise sources of the water and to present the complete picture.

The climb today to inspect the cisterns is more difficult, but more interesting, than the snake path. The walk to the foot of the rock is easy; but then begin a series of goat paths which crisscross the lower slopes. Parts have crumbled, and parts are blocked by boulders, and agility is needed to negotiate them. Eventually you find yourself at the mouth of one of the "holes," and looking through into the cavern is handsome reward for the effort.

There are four cisterns in the lower and eight in the upper

row. They are huge. The volume of the largest is 4,230 cubic meters and the volume of the smallest 2,500 cubic meters.

The plaster is indeed magnificent, beautifully applied and smooth to the touch, and looks as if it had been put on only a month before and not 2,000 years earlier. The water mark is still visible near the top, showing that the cisterns had often been almost full. The steps enabled the water to be reached when the level had dropped. You feel relieved that you are just a visitor and not an ancient "drawer of water." For the steps are narrow and are unprotected by a banister or rail. Just getting down and up, without the encumbrance of heavy water bags or jars, is work enough.

The cisterns were clearly scooped out of the cliff side by hand and were not natural caves plastered over. In a few places where the plaster has come away, the marks of the stonecutters may be seen. Moreover, in five of the cisterns, columns were left in the middle—that is to say that the rock was cut all around them, leaving them to support the roofs. In one cistern in the upper row, the largest of all, the column is twenty-five feet high and eight feet thick—twenty-five feet, of course, being also the height of the cistern. Nine cisterns are rectangular in shape; the others are irregular.

These, then, were the reservoirs that Herod's men had constructed. They were fed by aqueducts, the remains of which may be seen today. These are the traces of stone constructions at the level of the openings to the cisterns.

Where were the other ends of the aqueducts? To the north and south of Masada are two clefts in the mountains. They are called *wadis*, the local term for dry riverbeds. One aqueduct led from the southern wadi to the upper series of cisterns; the other water channel linked the northern wadi to the lower row.

There could be no doubt that these were the installations; and it was now known that the aqueducts were fed by water

Interior of one of the water cisterns. The original staircase is at right, foreground. Its size may be gauged by the figure in the background.

from the wadis. But how did the water get into the wadis? Where did it come from in this arid region?

From flash floods.

A flash flood is a sudden torrent of water that sweeps down the dry riverbeds and crevices that cut and scar the low-lying ground of the Dead Sea. It rushes down with great force and speed and in huge volume, filling the dry beds in seconds and bursting their banks, so that the area is flooded. The water comes from many miles away, either after a heavy downpour of rain in winter or melting snows on the distant mountain tops in spring. Water finds its own level, following the gradient from high ground to low. Where, as with the Dead Sea, the drop in altitude is sharp, the speed of the waterflow is rapid. What starts out as a trickle becomes a torrent.

It comes without warning. A few years ago, a party of French tourists were caught by a flash flood while walking through the canyon-like area of Petra, on the eastern side of the Dead Sea in Jordan. Most of them were drowned. The water rushed into the canyons so suddenly that it was over their heads before they had a chance to save themselves.

The waters mostly run to waste, and in a short time, baked by the hot sun, the ground shows almost no sign of having been moistened.

Herod's ingenious engineers who built the cisterns and aqueducts at Masada set out to harness the water, control it, and direct it into the rock-cut plaster-lined cavities. These would fill up in several hours, and there would usually be enough to last until the next flash flood.

To do this, they constructed dams in the two wadis and from the dams built the aqueducts, laying them along a careful course so that they sloped gently down to the mouths of the cisterns. When the waters came rushing through the wadis, they were held up by the dams, and then the aqueducts carried them by gravity flow to the scooped-out cisterns.

The 1955–56 expedition found no traces of a dam, but they

did find signs of a platform cut in the rock of the southern wadi to provide a place for a dam at the obvious site where it would have been located. "No big dam was needed," they wrote in their report, "as the valley at this point is rocky and narrow." South of the Roman ramp, this expedition also found a plastered strip of ruined aqueduct about one hundred and twenty feet in length and four feet wide. Their report says: "It was covered by a stratum of earth and stone rubble. The plaster is strong and rests upon a stone foundation; the built sides, which were constructed to keep the waters from descending the slope of the valley, are visible here and there."

This expedition thought the southern wadi was the only source feeding the cisterns. The Yadin teams found the northern wadi's link with the Herodian water system.

Here, then, were the reservoirs in the side of the cliff, which held the vast quantities of water for the dwellers on Masada. How did the water get to the top? It was carried, either by hand or by beasts of burden. In Herod's day, the job was no doubt done by slaves. Herod had many. In the time of the Zealots, they had to do it themselves, although they also may have been aided by animals. During the siege, they almost certainly had to do it under cover of darkness.

How, since the slope was so steep, did they reach the top? There seemed to be no sign of a path continuing up the northwestern face.

The archaeologists, however, found the answer. Running from both rows of cisterns across the western face toward the northern edge of the rock were man-built paths which then ran around the eastern slope to link up with the snake path.

What did they do with the water once it reached the top? This is where the cisterns cut in the summit came in. They were the storage "tanks" for daily use, and they held enough, with sparing use, to last for several weeks, if not months. They would probably be filled as soon as a flash flood filled the cliff-side cisterns. This perhaps also means that during the

Roman siege, the Zealots might not have needed to undertake the hazardous water-carrying journeys more than a few times. They were not as prodigal with water as was Herod—and the expedition soon discovered how lavish he was when they excavated the magnificent Roman-style baths on the summit, which he had constructed for himself and his household.

Today, with the aqueducts destroyed, the cisterns are empty, and the Yadin expedition, explorers of the twentieth century, had to resort to small bottles of water to quench their thirst, whereas 2,000 years ago others had stood here with access to tens of thousands of gallons, ingeniously brought by the wonders of their engineering.

The Hanging Palace

The three-tiered structure clinging to the northern point of the summit was the most striking building Herod's architects and engineers had erected at Masada. Why had he built it? What was its function? With which of the Herodian buildings described by Josephus could it be identified?

These were some of the questions this expedition hoped to be able to answer as they came to excavate Masada's breathtaking ruins. The object of the archaeologist is not to record, just for the sake of recording, the details of a wall, or a floor, or a column, or a jar, or a coin, but to use these finds, which may also be valuable and artistic in themselves, as clues to give an overall picture of the structure in which they were found or of which they were a part and the role they played in the lives of the people at the time.

We have already seen that some of the nineteenth century explorers had thought this northern building was a fort.

Aerial view of Herod's hanging palace on the northern edge of Masada. On the summit to the right of its upper terrace are the rectangular store-rooms, and adjoining them is the Roman-style bathhouse.

Visitors earlier in this century had realized that it was certainly not a fort but had not known quite what it was. It was Shmaryahu Guttman and Micha Livneh and the 1955–56 expedition who concluded quite positively that it was in fact the celebrated palace of Herod which Josephus had described. In so doing, they were challenging the conclusion of Schulten, who had said that Herod's palace was the large western building which he had briefly examined.

The conflicting opinions arose as a result of Josephus' description. Schulten's hypothesis was very feasible, for "his" building was indeed palatial; it was the largest building on Masada, and it was located at the most likely site for a palace. What had troubled scholars was that it did not meet the details in the record of Josephus.

Josephus had written that Herod "caused a sumptuous and magnificent palace to be erected . . . on the western slope, below the fortifications on the crest, and inclining in a northerly direction. . . ." True, the palace Schulten described was on the west, but it was not on the slope; it was not beneath the fortifications on the crest, but within the casemate perimeter; and it did not incline to, or face, the north.

Moreover, Josephus had added that "a sunken passage led from the palace to the hilltop, which was quite invisible from the outside." This did not at all match Schulten's building, which stood on level ground. It would not have needed a "sunken passage" to lead from the palace to the hilltop when it was already *on* the hilltop.

Only with the discoveries of the Israeli archaeologists in the middle fifties was it seen that this northern building *did* fit all except one of the details in Josephus. The one doubtful detail was Josephus' report that it was on "the western slope," whereas it is in fact right on the northern point. For the rest, the match was perfect. This building faced north; it was beneath the casemate; and the distance between the terraces was so great that a "passage" of some sort, preferably "invisible from the outside," was assuredly needed to link them and to get "from the palace to the hilltop," and such a passage —staircases—was found.

Even the "western slope" point, which seemed to be a contradiction, was explained by earlier scholars. Josephus had been mistaken, and they had a most feasible explanation as to why he had been wrong. He had never himself visited the actual site, they suggested, but had seen it only from a distance. Even his account of the siege by Silva was secondhand, for at the time he was already living in Rome. Nor indeed is it as detailed as his report of the siege of Jerusalem, where he was an eyewitness.

He says in his autobiography that as a youth he had spent three years in the Judean desert, and it is most probable that he saw the Masada fortress from the outside. At that time it was occupied by a Roman garrison, and it is unlikely that the soldiers would have allowed the young Jewish hermit, which he then was, to inspect the fortress buildings. "This impression is confirmed by all of Josephus' descriptions of Masada," says the 1955–56 report. "On the one hand he displays a good deal of knowledge, either his own or derived from authoritative eyewitnesses, and on the other he makes mistakes which show that he had not visited the site himself."

Now, the report says that, "the best view of the palace [i.e. this northern building] is obtained from the mountain west of Masada." Since "actually Masada has no north side, because the rock runs out there to a point . . . the spectator from the west sees the palace 'on the western slope . . . inclining to the north'—exactly as described by Josephus."

The report adds: "the rock-cut passage, invisible from the outside, seems to have left the greatest impression on contemporaries." The spectator from the west saw a large building on the lower terrace, then very much higher up a circular construction, and higher still, above a steep rock face, yet another building on the upper terrace. "The staircase between the [last] two buildings was cut in this rock and was hidden from the eye of the beholder. We may imagine the effects this 'sunk road' made on those outside when they saw a man disappear within the rock face and appear after some time on top of the rock."

If this was so, and Josephus' palace was this northern building and not the western one, which nowhere matched Josephus' description, what had those scholars to say who accepted Schulten's theory and what of Schulten himself? They were not quite happy about it, but they fell back on the argument that there were many inaccuracies in Josephus, and he had apparently been inaccurate here, too. But whereas the 1955–56 expedition had only had to explain away one inaccuracy—which they did in a most reasonable way—the others had to question his entire description. After the 1955–56 report, all accepted the fact that the palace described by Josephus was indeed this northern building.

In that case, what problem remained for this expedition to solve?

For one thing, much more excavating of the ruins themselves was necessary for all the archaeological facts to be established. For another, while this building might fit the description of Josephus, Yadin was nagged by the doubt that it did not seem like a functional palace. The Schulten building seemed more likely, yet it was not the building referred to by Josephus. It was Yadin's purpose thoroughly to excavate both and only thereafter to make a judgement.

At the conclusion of this work, Yadin was able to establish that *both* were palaces. The Schulten building was Herod's formal palace, the place where he conducted his official business, received visitors, carried out the ceremonies of royal protocol. The northern building, which was certainly the one described by Josephus, was Herod's private palace, his private villa if you like, the place to which he would retire with his friends and relax. To distinguish between the two, Yadin has called this the palace-villa and the other the western palace.

The upper terrace of the palace-villa is 65 feet above the middle terrace and 107 feet above the bottom terrace. When the expedition came to dig there they recognized that, in archaeological terms, this would prove the least interesting of the three. For since it was more exposed, it fell victim more readily to the ravages of the weather. And since it was more easily accessible than the others to anyone who reached the summit, both conquerors and occupiers in the distant past and visitors in recent years, it suffered greater damage, greater wear, and more looting.

Architecturally, however, it was most impressive. Here was a large terrace, virtually an extension of the summit, with a huge semicircular porch at the northern point which skirted the cliff edge, offering an all around view of the Dead Sea, the mountains, and the desert—and, of course, the remarkable projecting terraces below. At the back of the porch, closer to the summit, were the ruins of rooms. This terrace, Yadin concluded, was the dwelling part of the villa, the living quarters. They were not as large as earlier scholars had imagined. The latest archaeological results show that Herod had built four living rooms here and several corridors.

This is a good example of the value of extended archaeological research—whenever this is possible. The 1955–56 expedition, after their brief survey, reported finding "a rectangular house of nine rooms." Yadin's teams found that several of the "nine rooms" had in fact been built about five hundred years later by Byzantine monks. Masada had served as a retreat for such monks during the fifth and sixth centuries.

In some of the Herodian rooms, the archaeologists found mosaic floors, parts of which were in a good state of preservation. They were of simple geometric design, a hexagonal honeycomb pattern, in black and white. The white cubes were of local limestone and the black of a soft bituminous stone found near the Dead Sea. These are the earliest mosaics to be found in Israel. The pattern is the same as that of mosaics found in Italy belonging to the first century B.C. and first century A.D., which would definitely date the Masada works as Herodian even if there were no other evidence.

There were signs on the site itself that the walls and ceilings of these living rooms were also opulently decorated—not with mosaics but with paintings. The terrace had held elegant columns. These were no longer standing, but parts of them were found very close by. However, most of the column bases, column capitals, and chunks of the columns themselves, as well as portions of painted plaster that had once adorned the rooms on this terrace, were discovered by the Yadin expedition beneath a huge mound of earth and rubble immediately to the south of this upper terrace.

From the very beginning of the excavations, a large team had been assigned to excavate this mound, and the work was continued by successive teams throughout the entire two seasons of digging. Yadin estimates that altogether they shifted 40,000 cubic meters of debris. It was slow going, because, as always on the dig, all the debris was carefully put through sieves before being carted away. But the results were rewarding.

The purpose of this scrupulous study of the mound was not initially to find remains from the upper terrace but to investigate signs of a wall separating Herod's palace-villa from the rest of Masada. Protruding from the top of the earth mound were stones which suggested that they might be the top of such a wall; and indeed, after all the rubble was removed, there stood the wall, a Herodian wall, massive, beautifully preserved, covered by white stucco, a kind of plaster used for coating the surface of a building.

In the process of uncovering it, the volunteer archaeologists found such small but important items as ostraca, jewelry, and hundreds of coins, and—without sifting—pieces of fine orna-

Mosaic floor in one of the rooms of Herod's living quarters on the upper terrace of the hanging palace.

mental pottery of the Herodian period, as well as the parts of painted plaster and stone pillars we have already mentioned. The earth mound had probably started off as a rubbish dump, and the items from the upper terrace had been thrown there by those who had occupied Masada after Herod's day—the Zealots, the Roman garrisons, and the Byzantine monks.

A word about the stone columns, which Yadin suggests had probably been originally located on the semicircular porch as a purely decorative feature. Josephus, describing the magnificence of the palace, says that its pillars were cut from a single block—"each of one entire stone." Alas, archaeologists, by unearthing the reality, are often the enemies of the romantic. For what did Yadin's teams find? They found that each column had not been cut from a single stone but had been made up of several sections fitted together. Each section —and many of these were found intact—was shaped like a drum, or like a large round Swiss cheese. After they were put together, the whole column was fluted—vertical grooves cut out of its surface and running its entire length—and covered with stucco so that the joins would not be seen. It was then placed on a stone base and crowned with a decorative capital. In the upper terrace it was an Ionic capital, marked by a sculptured scroll-end on each side. Anyone seeing the columns even close up would get the impression recorded by Josephus.

Of greater archaeological significance were the marks found on the sections of the columns. To insure that each fitted snugly, and to facilitate easier assembly later, the stonemasons had given each a special marking, a letter to indicate the column to which it belonged, and a number to show its place in the column. The letters were Hebrew, showing that the expert masons and builders were Jews.

To get to the middle terrace, the expedition used the staircase which the Israel army engineers had constructed and not the original one built in Herod's day—although parts of that remained. Indeed, the lower staircase, linking the bottom terrace with the middle, was sufficiently preserved to show how it had been constructed. The whole of it had been built onto the rock and enclosed by an outside wall—which would have made it "invisible from the outside." The wall has long since crumbled and collapsed into the abyss below.

Since this staircase had to span a considerable height to the next terrace, and the whole structure clung to the edge of a cliff with no room for a normal sloping set of steps, Herod built a spiral staircase. Earlier archaeologists had found the plastered stone pillar around which the steps turned. The spiral stairs were approached by a few ordinary steps, and the excavations uncovered eight of these. They were of stone; but from pieces of charred wood and fragments of plaster found in the debris, the scholars concluded that above the stone steps there had been a spiral flight of wooden stairs. From other evidence they could presume that these steps had been wooden planks which rested on beams fixed with plaster to the walls.

Similar finds were made in the upper staircase, going from the middle terrace to the top, although here, only its lower section was preserved. The remains ran to a height of about twenty feet, and the stairs around three sides of it were stone. At the next turn were parts of a wooden step. However, unlike the lower staircase, which had been built *onto* the rock, this upper staircase was enclosed in a stairwell which had been scooped *out of* the rock. To any outside observer, the face of the cliff between terraces would appear undisturbed, and, of course, this "sunken passage" would have been invisible.

The chief feature of the middle terrace was the remains of

Iron staircase built by army engineers linking terraces of the hanging palace. In the distance (upper left) are the buildings of the expedition offices and base camp.

a round structure. This is what had led Lynch's companions in the nineteenth century to talk of "a round tower" and Tristram to mention "a strong circular fort with double walls."

Two low concentric walls took up most of the terrace. Their thickness was 3½ feet; the space between them 4 feet; and the diameter of the outer circular wall 48 feet.

At first glance, it was easy to see why the casual observer might have guessed that they were the original foundations of "a round tower," built to protect this northern edge of Masada. Later scholars, however, found that the top of the two circular walls were "built of straight, smoothed sandstone slabs." These, in fact, were the finished, smoothly leveled, rims of the walls. They had never been built any higher, certainly not of stone. The remains between the walls and in the center showed only that the space between the circles had never been filled in and that there were no marks to indicate that the structure had been roofed. What its function had been remained a puzzle.

Behind the concentric walls was a twenty-foot-wide porch and behind that, where the terrace met the Masada rock, an earlier experimental cutting had brought to light the remains of rooms, and, just below the peak of a huge pile of debris, the tops of four square stone pillars.

When the teams cleared away the mounds of rubble and the massive chunks of rock that had fallen from the upper level during the centuries, they found that the southern side of the terrace had originally been a roofed court. To its north and south were rooms which had been noticed during the earlier soundings. As for the pillars whose tops had been seen, these were columns attached to the southern wall which had partially supported the roof. The bottom part of the wall had been covered with decorative painting, but little of the paint remained.

Yadin reached the conclusion that this circular structure

was what is known in architecture as a *tholos*, a Greek word referring to a circular building, usually but not necessarily with columns supporting the roof. Such buildings were very popular in the Hellenistic world at the time. Resting on the top of the low concentric walls at Masada had been a floor, probably of wood.

As to why there had been two circular walls and not one, Yadin was able to explain this only after he had completed his excavation of all three terraces of the palace-villa and after studying the building methods of the ancient engineers. The problem they faced was how to provide enough support for the weight of the artificial terraces, constructed as they were at this narrow point of the rock. The steep face of the cliff left them no room for massive foundations. Herod had called for a *tholos*, but with the limited foundations they could provide, they were afraid that a single wall enclosing heaps of earth and stones would collapse. So they hit on the idea of concentric walls, with an empty space between them, which lightened the pressure. This is Yadin's theory, which is now generally accepted by scholars.

As to the function of the terrace, Yadin says that it was certainly designed by Herod as a place for rest and leisure, "a place where one could sit, eat, relax, and look at the view" —the same purpose as was served by the lower terrace.

The ancient engineers had been ingenious in providing supports for the top two terraces, but their full genius was applied to the construction of the bottom terrace, the most ornate and ambitious of the three. At this level, 107 feet below the summit, the northern edge of the cliff is at its narrowest, no more than a few yards wide. Yet what Herod wanted them to do was erect a terrace and build upon it a square structure, each side measuring 57 feet and lined with columns.

What they did, therefore, was to build walls at the edge of

View of the concentric walls of the "tholos" of the middle terrace. The square in the upper center of the picture is one of the Roman camps.

Middle terrace showing the supporting wall of the projecting upper terrace. (The protective rail on the upper terrace and at lower left of picture are recent installations.)

the proposed terrace and huge buttress walls right on the northern and eastern faces of the cliff, so that cliff and attached walls formed a compact mass to provide a solid platform for the buildings. Looking down at these walls from the edge of the terrace, clinging sheer to the almost perpendicular sides of the cliff, it is hard to imagine how this daring construction was carried out in those days.

There were some very interesting signs of how the builders of old had strengthened the attachment of the walls to the rock. Here and there on the face of the built walls were gaps of about nine inches between the stone slabs. On inspection, it was found that in some of them were the remains of thick branches of wood which had been set into plaster. Three of the gaps were directly in line with natural crevices in the rock against which the wall had been built. It was clear that the Herodian builders had used the branches as beams to "bond"—the building term for "binding together"—the wall to the rock, making use of the natural crevices in the cliff.

From the remains on this terrace it was possible to recapture the original design of the square colonnaded building, which had four porticoed cloisters—covered walks with columns on either side—surrounding a quadrangular open court. One wall, the southern, was formed by the face of the Masada cliff, the top of which formed the edge of the middle terrace. Thinking of the three terraces of the palace-villa, seen in profile, as huge steps, this southern wall would be the riser of the bottom step.

The walls and most of the columns of the exposed sides had long since collapsed and fallen into the depths below, but there was a large accumulation of debris on the southern side and along the west side of the court. When this was cleared, evidence was found that all parts of the building were plastered; that some of them carried a fine top coat which bore decoratively painted panels in a good state of preservation; that the columns, like those in the upper terrace, were made

A group of Corinthian capitals found among the debris.

not of a single stone but of drum-shaped sections; and that beneath the eastern and western cloisters were cellars and additional structures.

The columns, incidentally, stood on an Attic base, and unlike those in the upper terrace, were crowned with a Corinthian-style capital. An Attic base looks like three thick, flat, round biscuits, one on top of the other, the edge of the middle one being concave and of the other two convex. A Corinthian capital is bucket-shaped and adorned with carved acanthus leaves from which emerge two spiral scrolls, called *volutes*, stuck at an angle in the top corners and, at Masada, two smaller volutes rolled in toward each other and meeting in the center.

The wall paintings were varied. There were panels of green, striped with red, and bordered in red and black. Some were all red; and there were quite a number of "veined" murals, designed to give the effect of marble. Here, too, as with the columns, Herod's intention was to produce an imitation of opulence to impress visitors and friends, and as with the columns, he certainly succeeded in impressing Josephus many years later, for he wrote that marble covered the walls of the palace.

The paintings follow the style that was popular at the time in the Roman Empire and are among the best preserved of that period. Yadin was anxious, therefore, that their continued preservation should be safeguarded. What might normally happen at an excavation is that such treasures would be removed and placed on permanent exhibition at a museum. But because of the special attraction of Masada and the wish to enable visitors to see it as it was in antiquity, it was decided to keep the paintings where they were on the site.

A volunteer from France adds concrete to preserve loose plaster on one of the columns of the lower terrace. The column is topped by a Corinthian capital of the type used on the lower terrace.

The southern part of the lower terrace showing its columns and the beautiful frescoes discovered by the expedition.

A volunteer cleaning one of the frescoes of the lower terrace. The column above the fresco has an Attic base typical of those used on this terrace.

This, however, posed a problem. For centuries they had been protectively buried by accumulations of debris and before that by Herod's covered building. Now they were fully exposed to the weather, with the attendant dangers of erosion. Efforts had therefore been made to inject glue into the plaster backing so that it would adhere more firmly to the rock. But these were unsuccessful. Israel accordingly approached UNESCO, which has a department concerned with the preservation of historical sites, and also turned to Italian experts. Following their advice, the Masada wall paintings were carefully removed, most of the old plaster backing was scraped away, a new backing was applied, each painted panel was inserted in a special frame, and the framed paintings were restored to their original places in the lower terrace building. These are what may be seen on the site today.

The eastern structure adjoining the cellars beneath the building was a wing with several rooms. It was subjected to careful excavation by the Yadin scholars, and they made a remarkable archaeological discovery. They found that it housed Herod's private bath, and although comparatively small, it followed the classical pattern of a Roman bathhouse, complete with cold water pool, a tepid room, and a hot room with pipes coming up from the space between double floors.

Seeing this two-thousand-year-old structure, still quite well preserved, after visualizing the colonnaded building on the lower terrace and the concentric "pleasure *tholos*" of the middle terrace, gives a vivid impression of the personal luxury that Herod had ordered for himself and that his daring and imaginative engineers and architects had provided. It was clear, after eleven months of careful excavation, that this palace-villa had been built solely for the pleasure, comfort, rest, and relaxation of the king, and that the buildings, apart

Volunteers injecting glue into the plaster backing of frescoes to preserve them.

Frescoes and restored pillars as they appear today. The bars between the columns hold the protective glass which now covers the paintings.

Close-up of columns and glass-enclosed frescoes.

from the dwelling rooms on the upper terrace, were simply luxurious adornments.

Why had Herod chosen this particular northern site for his villa, where it hung over the precipice and required such effort and vast resources to build, when he could have chosen any flat site on the Masada summit? Yadin has an ingenious answer. It is the only site on the whole of Masada that gives shelter throughout the seasons from the searing sun and the hot wind. He writes:*

The northern point of the Masada rock—particularly the middle and bottom terraces—is the only site on Masada which is sheltered for most of the daylight hours: sheltered from the sun, so that it is cool and pleasant, and sheltered from the south wind—the rock walls of each terrace serve as windbreaks—so that it is always still.

How different from such luxurious living was the austerity of the Zealots a hundred years later, and how much more dramatic was the discovery of their poor remains than that of the structural riches of Herod.

Since the Zealots came later, their relics were discovered first by Yadin's diggers, for they lay in a stratum above the earlier levels. As the volunteers were scraping away and sifting the rubble on the lower terrace, before uncovering the stratum containing the wall paintings, they came across a thick layer of ashes. Examination showed that this was the result of a great fire.

Among the ashes were found date and olive pits as well as Jewish coins, belonging to the period of the Jewish War against the Romans, which had been struck between A.D. 66 and 70. Striking their own coins was the Jewish expression of independence. Some of the coins found in this stratum of the

---

* This and all other quotations from Prof. Yigael Yadin are taken from his *MASADA: Herod's Fortress and the Zealots' Last Stand*, Random House Inc., New York, 1966.

lower terrace carried the inscription *For the Freedom of Zion*. "It was clear," says Yadin, "that we were bringing to light the remains of that very fire mentioned by Josephus when he recorded that the fighters of Masada burned their communal buildings before they took their lives, to prevent their being used by the Roman conquerors."

The diggers' most dramatic find, however, was to come later, when they removed the debris from Herod's private bathhouse. On the steps leading to the cold water pool lay the remains of three skeletons. This would not normally occasion surprise. Human bones are frequently found at archaeological excavations; but when these were studied by anatomy experts, one was discovered to be that of a man in his twenties, one of a young woman, and one of a child.

All three were found in the Zealotian stratum. Next to the male skeleton were silvered scales of armor, arrowheads, parts of a Jewish prayer shawl *(talith)*, and an ostracon with a Hebrew inscription. The skeleton nearby had been identified immediately as that of a woman and needed no expert opinion: the skull still held the scalp, and attached to the scalp were beautifully plaited locks of brown hair. Next to the bones lay her sandals.

Yadin believes that the male skeleton was that of one of the Zealot commanders, and the others may have been those of his family. Recalling Josephus' report of their final night when the last survivor set fire to the king's palace and then killed himself at the side of his slain family, Yadin asks: "Could it be that we had discovered the bones of that very fighter and of his kith? This, of course, we can never know for certain."

In addition to excavating the wall that separated the palace-villa from the rest of the summit, the teams did a good deal of digging at its eastern end. It was here, when the wall was still buried beneath a mound of rubble, that the 1955–56 expedition had found an opening and next to it a stone bench. Scratched on the walls behind and at the side of the bench were primitive drawings, and in front of the bench were the remains of food—date kernels, nut shells, salt—and pieces of shoe leather, including soles and a thong. They concluded that the bench was used by a royal sentry, posted there to check entry to the villa, and that the drawings were the work of bored guards "whiling away the tedious hours of duty." The food remains suggested that some of them had munched on sentry duty and spat out the pits.

It was Yadin's theory that this entrance must have led to the staircase system of the villa. He was right. Excavation uncovered a broad flight of steps, and beneath them were the remains of an earlier set of steps. The obvious question was whether this was the work of the "Jonathan" whom Josephus had said was the first to build at Masada.

Elsewhere on this site there was additional evidence of two stages of construction. For the professional archaeologist the clues to two distinct building stages are usually easy to detect. At Masada, in the later construction, the building blocks were of a different size and the material used was limestone and not sandstone. It was also easy to see that a new supporting wall of rough stones covered the outer face of one of the original walls.

After lengthy and careful study, Yadin concluded that both stages belonged to the Herodian period, and the second stage may have been prompted by a change of architectural plan or by the earthquake which is known to have occurred during Herod's reign.

Actually, the expedition found no trace of any building belonging to the period before Herod—and they excavated ninety-seven per cent of the Masada summit; so there was no structural evidence to bear out Josephus' report of buildings and cisterns having been constructed prior to Herod by "Jonathan the High Priest." However, if, despite the lack of structural evidence, such buildings had existed, Yadin found one set of items that offer the clue to which of the two Hasmonean Jonathans Josephus was referring. They were numerous coins struck by Alexander Jannai. The "builder" would thus have been not Jonathan Maccabeus, who headed the Jewish Commonwealth from 160 to 143 B.C., as many scholars had supposed, but his grand-nephew, King Alexander Jannai, who reigned from 103 to 76 B.C., and who, as we have observed, was also known as "Jonathan the High Priest."

The Storerooms

The cluster of ruins to the immediate southeast of the palace-villa had long been identified by several nineteenth century explorers as the storehouses of Herod. They had reached this conclusion without excavation and without even a thorough examination. All they needed was a brief inspection, and they were right. These were the buildings that had been specially constructed by Herod during his fortification of Masada to house the stocks of food that would be needed if he ever had to use the place as a refuge.

Why had their recognition been so easy? The archaeological "detectives" had had two important clues to go on. One was contained in the historical record of Josephus. The other was in the shape and style of the buildings themselves, which were evident from the outline of their foundations and the rows of collapsed walls.

As to the written record, Josephus talks of the splendid buildings that were large enough to "store corn, wine, and oil in abundance, as well as pulses and dates, such as would enable men to subsist for a long time." It was known, therefore, that among the major group of structures erected by Herod were granaries and other large storage chambers. What was not

A section of the storerooms before excavation.

known until the first explorer reached the summit was whether any of their remains were still standing.

The report that they were was given by Wolcott in 1842. Armed with the clue from Josephus, he picked out this group of ruins, because of their shape. Their "peculiar form," he wrote, "composed of long parallel rooms, indicated that they had been storehouses or barracks, rather than private dwellings."

What he saw—and what was seen by visitors to the site for the next 120 years, right up to the time that this expedition started digging—was a large, well-defined area of ruins in the shape of a fat letter L as seen in a mirror (namely, with the upright arm on the right instead of the left). Or think of the area as filling three quarters of a large rough square, the bottom half consisting of a long rectangle and the top right hand corner a square. Each was clearly divided into a series of narrow, parallel oblongs, ten in the bottom, or southern, rectangular enclosure and four in the northern. Each oblong represented the foundations and parts of the walls of one storeroom. The space inside was filled with debris and the collapsed stones from the upper part of the walls.

The storerooms in the northern series were each about 65 feet long and 12 feet wide. The southern ones were larger—averaging 90 feet by 14 feet. Separating the two series was a 20-foot-wide path, and running around three sides of the complex was a path 10 feet wide.

I mentioned that it was comparatively easy for scholars to recognize them as storehouses, certainly for later scholars familiar with ancient Greek and Roman architecture as brought to light at archaeological excavations. As a matter of fact, certain features of the Masada storerooms matched the recommendations for standard storehouse construction by the first century B.C. Roman architect and engineer, Vitruvius (Marcus Vitruvius Pollio), in his ten-volume work *De Architectura*. He and others suggested, for example, that openings to the rooms should be made on the north side—probably to shield the food from the sun. At Masada, all the southern group of storerooms have such northern openings. They also recommended that the storehouses be built on high ground. This is followed at Masada: the northern section is the highest part of the summit.

Visitors today do not see the ruins as Wolcott and his successors saw them but rather as they were seen by Eleazar ben Ya'ir and Herod before him; for most of the storehouses have been restored. The debris was removed during the months of excavation; the interiors of the storerooms were excavated down to their original floors; the walls of some of them were built up to their original height of eleven feet, with a black-painted line marking the division between what had remained of the old wall below and the newly restored part above; and the paths between the storerooms, between the northern and southern group and around the enclosures, were cleared.

For the volunteers who arrived toward the end of the second season of excavations, the restorations offered a sight unusual at an archaeological dig. Normally an archaeologist looks at ruins and tries to visualize what they were like in olden times. Now, however, the volunteers could see what they had looked like originally, and it was hard to visualize what they had looked like in their ruined state.

But to help them and future visitors, Yadin had deliberately left a few storerooms completely unrestored, had not built up all the walls to their original height, and had insisted on the black dividing line to show what was original and what was new. It was just as well that he did; for the restoration work was so authentic that without the line it would have been difficult to tell the distinction.

It was a happy, and archaeologically rare, decision to restore during the excavation, and to begin with this complex of storerooms. They had been built of stone, large slabs weighing 400 and 500 pounds—and this made the job at once simpler and more difficult. Simpler, because being stone, they lasted without crumbling throughout the centuries, and being heavy, they remained on the site when the walls collapsed, so that they could now be reused to build the walls anew. More difficult, because their weight made it necessary to bring up heavy equipment to the summit to lift them, and this in itself was a problem. It was solved by dismantling the equipment below, sending up the sections by cable rail, and reassembling them on top.

Another factor that eased the restoration task on this site, where the typical storehouse architecture had called for so many long thick walls, was that their ruined state had been caused not only by Zealot destruction but by subsequent earthquake. This meant that in some cases the walls collapsed not into a higgledy-piggledy heap—although they sometimes did— but into neat rows of stone slabs. This made it somewhat easier to tell which stone belonged to which row and which row to which wall.

Yadin was determined that the restoration should be absolutely true to the original, and the work was carried out under his supervision. It was so carefully done that while not every stone was put back in the position from which it had fallen, it *was* replaced in the wall to which it had originally belonged.

With the space between the walls thus cleared, the excavations could begin. There was no problem here of identification of the ruins, though despite Wolcott's published judgment, a few later explorers in the nineteenth century had put forward the mistaken view that they were Herod's palace. Nevertheless, the challenges were considerable. The expedition would be the first to carry out a thorough dig. Since the storerooms must have played a central part in the lives of whichever community had occupied the summit, the remains might shed much light on the lives of the Zealots. It was with great eagerness that Yadin followed the work of removing the stones and then the careful scraping away of the debris by the early group of volunteers, coming closer each day to the level of the original floors.

After excavating to a depth of some three feet, the archaeologists came upon a stratum of destruction. This was a thick level of ashes, among them chunks of charred beams. Here was the result of Zealot destruction. They had set the buildings on fire before taking their lives. The beams were those of the roofs which had collapsed in the blaze.

Also scattered among the ashes were the pieces from hundreds of broken vessels. Yadin was wise enough to examine them carefully where they lay before ordering their removal, and this enabled him to reach an interesting—and unusual—conclusion. At a normal archaeological site, a feasible deduction would be that whatever vessels had been on the floor would naturally have been shattered when the roof fell on them. But here, a detailed inspection of the position and the state of the sherds revealed that the vessels had been deliberately broken. Quite clearly, said Yadin, before setting fire to the storerooms to deny their use by the Romans, the Zealots had smashed their storage vessels.

When the sherds were washed—some of them bore inscriptions in Hebrew—tagged, as usual, with the particular area storeroom in which they were found, and submitted to the skillful hands of the pottery restorers, the archaeologists were able to deduce the storage system used by the Zealots, the food they stocked, certain religious customs they followed, and the date of the vessels.

Oil was kept in large containers of a special shape. Wine was stored in differently shaped jars. Vessels for flour had yet another shape. Each storeroom stocked only one type of food. One room held only wine jars, another only oil, and so on. In none were the vessels mixed.

From their shape and make, many of the containers were found to be Herodian and were later taken into use by the

Various types of pottery vessels, some reconstructed, found during the excavations.

Zealots, who marked them with Hebrew inscriptions. Several bore Hebrew names.

Perhaps the most important inscriptions were those consisting of a single Hebrew letter. This was the Hebrew equivalent of the letter T, and it was found on several jars. This stood for, and was the initial letter of, the Hebrew word *truma*—the dues from field produce which, under ancient Jewish law, were contributed to the priests. Elsewhere on Masada, a jar was discovered bearing the Hebrew inscription *Ma'asser Cohen*, which means "tithe (or tenth part) for the priest." In olden times, no observant Jew would eat food unless it came from stocks out of which the *truma* and *ma'asser* had been deducted and set aside as priestly dues. It was thus possible to conclude that the Zealots were equally devout in their religious duties, highly orthodox Jews who were strictly faithful to their religious laws even under siege, when every grain of flour was precious, and even under the pressures of battle.

At the entrance to one of the storerooms the archaeologists came upon scores of coins scattered on the floor. As Yadin looked at them and noticed their spread, it seemed to him that they lay as they would if someone had deliberately flung them on the ground. It is his theory that as the end came, the man in charge of the stores had taken the less precious coins from his till and thrown them away. This, of course, is in keeping with the firm evidence of the charred beams and the broken vessels that the Zealots carried out a deliberate destruction before taking their lives.

What were the coins used for? Not for "money" in the normal sense, for there was no buying and selling on Masada, no trading or commercial dealings. They were almost certainly brought by the Zealots when they left Jerusalem, and Yadin suggests that they were probably used on Masada as tokens in the food rationing system that was assuredly in effect during the siege, serving as a form of "ration cards." This would also explain why there had been such a stock in the storerooms area and similar collections in the ruins of other communal buildings on the summit.

The coins in the storerooms, and those found scattered on the floors of other public buildings, were of bronze. They were thus of little intrinsic value, and so no effort was made to keep them from the Romans. The more precious silver coins had been hidden, and hidden well, for they were found only nineteen centuries later when the Yadin expedition started excavations. Today, of course, even the bronze coins are valuable. They belong to A.D. 67 and 68. Not that they are so marked. The marking is *Year Two* and *Year Three*. These refer to the second and third years of the Jewish revolt against the Romans, which began in A.D. 66. Coins were struck by the Jewish authorities throughout the five years of this war up to the fall of the Temple and of Jerusalem in A.D. 70, and they bear the number of the year in which they were minted, from *Year One* to *Year Five*.

Did the excavations in the storerooms furnish any proof one way or the other of whether the Zealots had deliberately left stocks of food untouched? It may be remembered that toward the end of Eleazar ben Ya'ir's final address, as reported by Josephus, he called upon his people, before taking their lives, to "let us first set fire to the fortress and to our possessions; and thus the Romans, neither taking us prisoners nor finding anything to loot, will even regret the possession of the place. One thing only let us spare—our store of food: to serve as a proof that we were not driven to this violent procedure by famine, but maintained our first resolution of dying rather than submitting to slavery."

The expedition found, as we have seen, that there had been deliberate destruction both of storerooms and jars of food. But they also found a few storerooms in which there was no sign of fire, no sign of destruction, and no vessels whatsoever. This suggested that these rooms had remained intact—and their food stocks, too. The Romans would thus have got the message—as

Bronze coins of the time of the Jewish revolt among those found in the storerooms and other public buildings. They bear the inscription "For the freedom of Zion."

well as the food—consumed the stores and removed the un-broken vessels. It is Yadin's judgment, as he writes, that "in order to achieve their purpose, the Zealots did not need to leave *all* their stores of food to the Romans. It was enough for them to leave one or two rooms with untouched victuals to show that they had not died through lack of food. It is pos-sible that the undamaged storerooms which we unearthed were the very rooms in which the Zealots had left food, which was later eaten by the Roman garrison."

Adjoining the storeroom complex to its immediate west lay the ruins of a large, almost square, Herodian building, with rooms ranged around a central courtyard. The recent excava-tions suggest that this served as the administrative center of Masada. Only toward the end of their dig did the scholars find the ruin of a most interesting structure beneath the rubble of the central court—a ritual bath.

With most of the debris cleared from storerooms and ad-ministration building and the restoration under way, Yadin surveyed the scene and said to himself—and then to his teams—that there must have been a gate or entrance to this sector of Masada. This was, after all, probably the most important area on the summit, containing the palace-villa of the king, the food stores, and the arms stores.

Josephus had written that Herod had stocked Masada not only with food but also with weapons of war. However, these had been taken by the Jewish commander who captured Masada at the beginning of the Jewish revolt. Whatever weapons the Zealots had used—mostly bows and arrows, some of which were found elsewhere on the summit—would not have been left in the armory during the siege but distributed to the various defense posts. At all events, the recent expedi-tion discovered none in the storerooms.

Entrance to this section, decided Yadin, must certainly have been controlled. When he saw the restored walls going up, he thought he knew where that entrance would have been. For with the walls up, one could no longer reach the storerooms as it had been possible to do before the excavations began— simply by stepping over the rubble. Now it was evident that the only opening lay near the northwestern corner of the administration building.

When he reached this conclusion, the "opening" was a mound of debris and fallen boulders, and he ordered his team to start clearing and excavating. They did. True enough, they found a fine Herodian gate, complete with an L-shaped stone bench and parts of the backing walls. As Yadin writes: "A single watchman posted here could check all who entered and left this important compound of storehouses."

The Roman-style Baths

There was one more ruin in the area of the storehouses, although obviously not itself a storeroom, which had long interested scholarly visitors to the region. The remains were those of a roughly square structure, filling the space in the northwest corner of the storeroom complex but tilted at a slight angle to it.

Several earlier explorers had expressed the thought that it must have had something to do with the storehouses. They were mistaken. What had led them astray was not only the position of the ruin but the recognizable shape of part of it. Visible among the heaps of rubble and debris were the remains of a large chamber, almost squarish, each side more than thirty feet long, and for an ordinary room unusually thick walls— six feet. Their conclusion was understandable. This, they said, was no doubt a watchtower or a defense tower guarding the storerooms and the approach to the palace-villa. A few thought that it may have been an administrative building associated with the central stores.

The Yadin expedition expected no surprises when they began removing the huge piles of debris; but soon, with some of the rubble from the large room cleared, more of the inside walls were exposed, and these were carefully examined. What the archaeologists were amazed to find were impressions in the plaster of oblong clay pipes. When they dug further, they came across parts of the pipes themselves still in their original position near the bottom of one of the walls. More pieces of piping were found in the debris.

It was clear that these wall pipes belonged to a building that had nothing to do with towers or administration or stores. This was obviously the hot room of a typical, classical, Roman-style bathhouse. The idea of such a specially built structure on so remote and unlikely a spot as the desert height of the Masada rock fitted well with Herod's overall conception of raising a magnificent royal citadel.

The archaeologists kept digging with even more excitement, anxious now to see whether any of the standard features of a Roman hot room were preserved. They were. After reaching part of the floor level, they probed beneath it. Sure enough, they found another floor, and in the space between the two were numerous small pillars or piers, close together—more than two hundred of them! They were made of round clay bricks and were very well preserved. These small piers were common in the underground heating chamber of a Roman hot room, serving as supports for the upper floor.

There could now be no doubt whatsoever as to the identity of this chamber. It followed from this that the rooms next to it, not yet excavated, were assuredly the usual additional ones found in Roman baths: the cold room, the tepid or warm room, and the disrobing room. There was also a court.

The court was known about—although not its function. It had been noted by the 1955–56 expedition. It occupied the northern half of the building and was largely rectangular in shape, 60 feet long and 27 feet wide. The southern half, said

Two views of the hot room (caldarium) *of the Roman-style public baths. Left: Its original floor, of which only a fragment remains (center foreground, on wooden slat), rested on more than 200 of these small pillars. The space beneath this floor, housing the pillars, formed the* hypocaust, *or heating chamber. The niche in the rear holds the remains of the original hot tub.*

the expedition, contained four rooms, but again they were unable, owing to limited time, to say what these were.

Yadin had now found the answer. The hot room was the largest of the four and turned out to be 36 feet by 33. He could thus tell his teams what to expect as they proceeded to excavate the other three.

Roman bath buildings were planned for the following procedure: The bather entered the *apodyterium*, the undressing room, where he left his clothes. In the large public baths, he would then go to the *unctorium*, the "oiling" room, where he would be anointed with oil, and from there to the court or another room to perform exercises. From there he would go to the *caldarium*, the hot room, and from there to the *sudatorium*, the steam room. In the smaller baths, as at Masada, there was no separate *unctorium*, so the bather would proceed, after undressing, to the hot room. Nor was there a separate *sudatorium* at Masada, and indeed the *caldarium* and *sudatorium* were often combined in a single room.

From the hot room the bather went to the *tepidarium*, the tepid or warm room, to cool off gradually, so this was usually an elaborate lounging room. From here he entered the *frigidarium*, the cold room, which was usually a pool of cold water.

The open space below the floor which allowed the hot air to pass through and thus heat the room above was known as the *hypocaust*. This, at Masada, was where the many small pillars had been found. The Romans, in olden days, used the *hypocaust* not only in their baths but also to heat rooms in private houses, particularly in the colder northern provinces. At one end of the hot room, usually set in an apse, a semicircular niche, was the *labrum*, the cold tub. At the opposite end of this room was the *alveus*, the hot tub.

This, then, was the usual design in Roman bath construction.

At Masada, the expedition found that in the hot room not much of the top floor remained; but the part that was preserved was tiled in black and white, forming a geometrical design. Yadin noted that here, too, as in the palace-villa, there had been two stages of construction, and in the earlier stage, the upper floor had been decorated with mosaics. The later floor was paved with black and white tiles. The same was true of other rooms in the bathhouse.

Apart from this remaining piece of floor, the main objects unearthed by the excavators were row upon row of tiny pillars upon which the upper floor had rested. The bottom floor on which they stood—as upright as on the day they were installed —was intact. The impressions on the plastered walls of the clay pipes were clearly visible, and so, of course, were parts of the pipes themselves, which were still attached to the wall in a corner.

In the northern wall of this hot room was the apse, and pieces of quartz were found there that were certainly parts of the cold bath. In the opposite wall was a rectangular niche which held the remains of the hot water tub.

This is how the hot room operated. From an outside stove, hot air was channeled into the space between the two floors. From there it rose up the clay pipes in the walls of the almost unventilated room, emerging both from openings at the top of the pipes and from holes in their sides. To turn the *caldarium* into a *sudatorium*, water would be dashed on the hot floor to produce steam. Cold water for the quartz tub came from the outside through a lead pipe, and parts of this pipe were found by the teams.

Of this hot room, its plan and technical arrangements, Yadin wrote: It "is not only identical with that of other bathhouses (less well-preserved) of the Herodian period discovered both at Jericho and Herodion but is almost exactly like the handsome Roman bathhouses of Pompeii and Herculaneum."

The hot room led to the adjoining tepid room. Although much smaller—about one third of the size of the hot room—it was more elegantly decorated. It had frescoes, for example, and these were similar to the wall paintings found in the palace-villa. Its floor, as in the hot room, was paved with black and white tiles, only smaller. None was found in place, although their impressions on the cement in which they had been embedded were very clear. A few broken ones were discovered among the debris. As for the rest, it is Yadin's theory that such expensive tiles were probably taken by the Roman soldiers when they left.

The next room, entered from the tepid room, was the smallest of them all, just about half the size of the *tepidarium*. This was the *frigidarium*. There was nothing elaborate about this cold room, for the ancient bathers spent little time here—just in and out of the icy water. It consisted of a miniature swimming pool, with steps along one side leading from the top to the bottom. Pool and steps were well-preserved and were plastered with the same waterproof material which had been used in the rock-cut cisterns.

Alongside the tepid and cold rooms, and as large as the two together, was the undressing room, the *apodyterium*. From the remains, it was apparent that this had been as elegantly decorated as the tepid room—and for the same reason: much time was spent in both. The floor had also been paved in black and white tiles, and the walls were frescoed.

There was evidence here that originally the ceiling had also been decorated. In the debris, pieces of painted plaster were found, which had clearly come from the collapsed ceiling, and this pointed to the probability that the ceilings in the other rooms had been adorned in the same way. These paintings were artistically superior to those in the palace-villa and were of different design, following geometric and floral patterns.

In a corner of this room, the archaeologists came across a small reservoir that had obviously been added later. For one thing, it did not "belong" in a classical disrobing room. For another, it had been built upon the original floor tiles, and its walls covered parts of the frescoes. Excavations elsewhere in the room unearthed a bench which also covered part of the floor paving and the plastered walls; and this bench was made of sections taken from Herodian columns. Such alterations and additions were the work partly of the Zealots and partly of the Roman garrison that followed them.

Excavation of the large courtyard showed that originally it had been partly covered, with columns supporting the roof and a decorated lintel between them. Some of these columns were still standing. Also found were parts of the lintel, some scattered in the debris and some, as Yadin wrote, in positions where they had "been used by the Zealots or the Roman troops to repair the oven of the baths." He adds: "This is a good example of what has frequently happened in many ages—where the architectural ornaments of one period were later used as common building materials without any relation to their decorative feature."

Clearance of the court also brought to light parts of a mosaic floor. The materials used and the design were exactly the same as those in the mosaics of the palace-villa's upper terrace—a hexagonal honeycomb pattern in black and white. Yadin considers this of great significance in fathoming the history of Herod's buildings. For, taken together with the frescoes found in two of the rooms, it showed, he wrote, "that the bathhouse and at least the upper terrace were built during the same stage of construction," and the works of art, mosaic and painting, were done by the same artists.

We mentioned at the beginning of this section that the entire building was set at a slight angle to the storerooms. This seemed odd at first; but when, in the course of excavations, it was possible to prepare accurate architectural plans, what was immediately noticeable was that the bathhouse was in perfect alignment with the upper terrace. "There is no doubt," concluded Yadin, "that it formed part of the complex of handsome buildings which Herod erected here for himself and his family, as well as for the garrison he had with him."

Of the building itself, he wrote later: "What we had excavated turned out to be one of the most beautiful and complete examples of a Roman bathhouse, among the most ancient ever discovered in the country and the region."

The Working Palace

The large building about midway along the western edge of the summit was the one which the archaeologist Schulten had dubbed the palace of Herod *as described by Josephus.* He had been mistaken, and this was understandable, for he had made only a brief survey, although it is amazing how much he managed to crowd into those few hours. The 1955–56 expedition spent a few days here, too short for a thorough dig but long enough to establish that it had been *a* but not *the* Herodian palace—and long enough to spot some other errors of their predecessors.

One of them was Schulten's "discovery" in one of the wings of traces of a raised bench running along a wall inside a room which opened onto a court. On the basis of this, he suggested a theory about the architecture and function of this wing of the building. The 1955–56 expedition decided to put this theory to the test by doing a trial dig at that particular spot. The "bench" turned out to be nothing more than—in the words of their report—"a purely accidental higher accumulation of debris along the wall!"

To do Schulten justice, he, too, would have discovered that his first thought had been mistaken if he had had the time to dig. But it was an amusing warning to archaeologists—and indeed to any scholar—not to go off half-cocked before completing a thorough study. Mistaking debris for structure reminds me of a cynical friend who once playfully charged a Middle Eastern archaeologist with trying to "decipher" a wiggle etched in a tablet, because he believed it to be a phrase in an ancient tongue, when it was only a crack in the stone!

Schulten hazarded a guess about another wing of the building, which consisted of a series of rooms around a central courtyard: he thought it had been a harem! There is a sober footnote on this in the report of the 1955–56 expedition: "It is doubtful if Herod was accompanied on his probably rare visits to Masada by a female entourage requiring so many rooms." Yadin's findings show that Schulten was nearer the truth.

Incidentally, the 1955–56 expedition thought it was used as barracks. Yadin found—although we are anticipating—that it was the service wing of the palace.

When the Yadin expedition had started excavating, they had known the general plan of this huge building both from the brief reports of the few earlier surveys and from what they could see of the ruins themselves. It was evident that it consisted of three main wings: a rectangular western wing, lying north to south, closest to the casemate wall; a rectangular eastern wing, parallel to it; and a southern wing, almost square, adjoining and in line with the southern part of the western wing and cutting into the southern part of the eastern rectangle.

Excavation here was particularly difficult. Facing the archaeologists were mounds of rubble and heaps of large stones, stones too heavy for manual clearance. They eventually had to bring up cranes to remove them. Yadin assigned a large body of volunteers to this area, an average of sixty from each two-week group working throughout both seasons of the expedition.

The throne room was found in the southern wing, the one that was almost square. The entire wing consisted of rooms ranged around a quadrangle, and from their shape, their installations, their decorative features, the objects found in them, it was clear that this was the main residential wing of the palace.

Part of the working palace looking toward the southeast.

The throne room was different from the rest—a chamber on its own in the southeast corner. It had three entrances; access to it from the court was through a hall, and at the entrance to the hall stood two painted pillars. But the "clincher" that this really was the throne room were four rectangular hollows in the floor, covered, like the floor, with plaster, and evidently designed to hold the feet of a throne or the tips of canopy poles.

During excavation, as the diggers approached the level of the floor, they found a thick layer of ashes, the product of the fire when the Zealots burned the building. Among the ashes were shattered fragments of handsome vessels made of bronze and bone.

However, what had clearly been the most richly adorned room in the palace was the entrance hall to the throne room. The finest mosaic in Masada was unearthed here.

The discovery followed weeks of ant-like labors by the volunteers in removing the debris. As they neared the floor level, they began to come across colored cubes scattered here and there. This meant two things: One, that the floor had originally been decorated with a colored mosaic—the first time a colored mosaic had been encountered at Masada. The second was that it had obviously suffered some destruction, for otherwise the cubes would not be out of place. Whether anything had been preserved would be known only when they reached floor level.

As the work proceeded, Yadin seldom left the site. Eventually the floor came into view. There, after the whisk brushes had done their job, stood revealed the prize. The destruction had been confined to just over half the floor. The remaining part, in an excellent state, was decorated with one of the earliest colored mosaic floors discovered in the country and the most beautiful of the period. Its several borders were of geometric design, but the central decoration depicted plant life frequently found in Jewish art, like olive branches, pomegranates, and the leaves of the fig and the vine, beautifully executed.

Incidentally, this mosaic had not been damaged when the Zealots fired the building. Yadin says that the destruction of part of it came much later and was probably the work of men seeking treasure thought to be hidden beneath the floor.

What we have called the east wing, really adjoining the northeast portion of the residental wing, had a similar architectural design, namely, rooms built around a central court. These, however, were smaller rooms, with different installations, and it was clear that this was the service wing of the palace. The two together formed a structure of outstanding luxury. The kitchen alone could serve up a banquet for numerous guests. Huge stoves were found, belonging to the Herodian period, each of which could hold twelve cooking pots.

Among the private service chambers the archaeologists found a small bathhouse, complete with cold water pool and a room for a hot bath. The floor of this bathroom was covered with a mosaic; and so was the floor of the corridor leading to it! This, too, was done in colored stone, and most of it is very well-preserved, but it is not as handsome as the one in the hall near the throne room.

The part that is not well-preserved is the part on which some crude building work had been done at a later period. These are the remains of what may have been a stove or a closet which had been added by the Zealots. This, writes Yadin, is "one of the features that underline again and again the startling contrast between the Masada of Herod and the Masada of the beleaguered Zealots during the revolt." The Zealots had built these additional furnishings for their needs and not given a thought to the ornamentation that was spoiled in the process.

A volunteer from Holland cleaning part of the border of a mosaic floor.

Seeing these discoveries on the site as they were found, the remains of Herod together with the remains of the Zealots, makes very real the characters of both and the totally different spirit that moved them.

The third wing, on the west, held the private storerooms of the palace, with administrative quarters in its northern section. These storerooms, built to the same long and narrow design as the central storehouses, though of different dimensions, made the palace independent for its supplies. In Herod's day, they also contained stocks of exotic items not found in the central stores, for among the debris the archaeologists discovered broken fragments of numerous small flasks that had contained cosmetic oil.

During the period of the Zealot revolt, it is Yadin's judgment that the palace was used as administrative offices and its private storerooms held specially conserved food which was nutritious, concentrated, easy to ration, and easy to eat. It was the discoveries themselves that led him to this conclusion. A thick layer of ashes covered the floor of the largest of the storerooms—the Zealots had set fire to the building—and among the ashes were hundreds upon hundreds of broken jars. Most of them bore such Hebrew inscriptions as "pressed figs" and "dried figs." This would have been an ideal food for distribution and consumption during the siege.

This was Herod's official, "working" palace, spacious, sumptuous, expensively decorated, and independent. It also possessed its own small cistern which unlike the other reservoirs at Masada, was filled by rainwater collected from roofs and courts and channeled to it. Here at the palace Herod con-

Part of the small private bathhouse in the working palace. The floor decoration is a colored mosaic.

Two views of the elegant polychrome floor at the entrance to Herod's private bath. In the foreground is a crude stove or closet built later by the Zealots.

ducted his business whenever he visited Masada and here too, he maintained his official residence. When he wished to relax, he would proceed to his private palace-villa, his "country residence," a few hundred yards away. There were all the amenities of royal living in both.

Nearby, five smaller buildings were found, lying southeast and south of the large palace. All were built at the same time as the palace, and all followed the same architectural design as its residential wing, namely, rooms built around a quadrangle. Wall paintings were found in one, identical with those in the palace-villa. Yadin believes these were small palaces—really villas—built by Herod for members of his immediate family.

The excavations showed that during the Zealot period, they had housed numerous families. This was evident from the walls and partitions that had been added to the buildings so that each family could have its few square yards of privacy.

One of the sites marked out for excavation before the expedition started its work was a rubble-piled ruin just to the southeast of the large palace. No previous explorer had known what it was, just as none had known about the Roman-style bathhouse. There was nothing about its shape to offer a clue. So the only thing to do was to clear the stones and start digging.

They dug and dug. They soon came to the outside walls, but in the large area in the center there was nothing, none of the walls of rooms that would be expected in a normal building. When they went on digging, they found out why. What they had excavated was a huge swimming pool or public bath, enclosed by fine stone walls, with a set of broad, well-plastered steps at one end. A number of built-in hollows in the walls baffled the diggers until Yadin came up with the ingenious theory that they were used by the bathers to leave their clothes. Zealot remains, including coins, found on the site, show that the pool was in use in their day, too.

The archaeologists had fun with the next ruin in this area, further south. Among the debris were parts of collapsed walls, and these were marked by rows of small cells or niches. These were examined by Yadin and his colleagues before excavations began, as they had been by scholars before him, but without digging he could reach no definite judgment. Scholarly opinion was divided. Some said the original building must have been a pigeon cote, the pigeons playing a role in some kind of religious rite or being kept for their droppings which were used as fertilizer. Others held that it was a columbarium, a building with tiers of niches to hold the urns of cremated bodies.

Yadin kept an open mind as he ordered digging to commence, although he had doubts about the pigeon cote theory. For one thing, inspection of the broken sections of wall showed that they belonged to a fine building—too handsome for birds. For another, the niches seemed to him to be small for pigeons or doves.

What came to light was a round building with a wall across its diameter, which had an opening in the middle. The niches were in straight rows on the inside of the circular wall and both sides of the dividing wall. It was constructed in the Herodian period, but there was evidence that it had been used both in the time of the Zealots and several hundred years later during the Byzantine period. The Byzantine monks, indeed, had built a new floor, above the level of the original floor, and their remains, including Byzantine sherds, were found in their stratum.

The practical Yadin decided on a simple test for the bird theory. The chief mason to the expedition happened to be a

Two views of the public bathing pool just southeast of the working palace. The broad steps bear the original plaster. The niches in the outer wall may have been used by bathers to put their clothes. Above: The wavy black line on the nearest wall marks off the restored section from the original part of the wall as found by the archaeologists.

pigeon fancier and breeder, and he was asked to bring one along when he returned from his weekend at home. He did, and on Sunday morning the diggers solemnly walked to the circular building and watched while the mason tried to thrust his bird inside one of the niches. It was not a fat bird. It was rather small, in fact; but try as he would, he could not get it in. The niches were too small.

It was Yadin's theory that the building was a columbarium. But since cremation is not customary among orthodox Jews, he thinks Herod had it built for the remains of his servants and members of his court who were not Jewish.

The Find in the Square Building

The remaining Herodian ruin on the summit, apart from the perimeter wall, was a large square building just south of the central storerooms. The outlines alone suggested that it must have been a stately structure in olden times. As with several other structures on Masada, it, too, had a rectangular central court; but unlike them, instead of single sets of rooms ranged around the court, only one side held single rooms; in the others the rooms were two deep. On one side they were three deep, but Yadin noted that the third row was not Herodian; it had been added by the Zealots.

Also unusual were the constructions in the court itself. Earlier scholars had suggested that they may have been erected by the Roman soldiers who occupied Masada after Herod's death, for it was evident that they had been built later than the main building. This expedition found that they had been constructed *very* much after Herod—some five hundred years later, in fact! They were Byzantine.

The early Schulten, simply looking at the ruins of this square building, thought it had been a "small palace." Later scholars thought it had been built by Herod to house the royal

The columbarium *with its tiers of niches which held the burial urns.*

guards; and since the rooms fronting on the court were large and the rear ones small and of identical size, they offered the suggestion that the large rooms were for the officers and the small ones for the men.

Yadin thinks this is possible. However, he found that each large room was linked to two small rooms, and the three rooms comprised a single dwelling unit. The entire building thus consisted of a series of identical three-room apartments. It may have held a garrison. Yadin thinks it more likely that it had been intended by Herod for his chief administrators or officials. Since he cannot be certain, he has called it "The 'Apartment' or Garrison Building."

Although the revelation of even a tiny detail of some ancient structure is of absorbing interest to the professional archaeologist, it was not the uncovering of this square building that caused the greatest excitement among the expedition. What did quicken their pulse was a discovery associated with the Zealots.

Among the debris in the apartments were such remains as handsome alabaster vessels, which suggested that during the Jewish revolt this building housed some of the Zealot leaders and their families. But the prize find occurred beneath the floor of a large room in one of the dwelling units. Carefully working their way through the original floor level, the lucky volunteers assigned to this section of the site were suddenly amazed to come across a heap of coins stuck together.

Yadin, "aware," as he writes, "of unusual movement" in this area, did not wait to be called but raced over, and when he got there, the volunteers were still "staring fascinated" at what they had uncovered. Yadin, too, stared at the coins "and from the color of the mold clinging to them it was clear that these were coins of silver. Bits of cloth still stuck to part of the heap," Yadin continues, "and it was evident that the coins had originally been placed in a special bag and hidden beneath the floor."

Silver shekels and half-shekels as they were found.

There was equal excitement after they had been removed with the most diligent and loving care and cautiously cleaned —in the expedition laboratory, not at the washstands. What then lay revealed was a veritable archaeological treasure: thirty-eight silver shekels and half-shekels, in mint condition, struck during the years of the revolt, several in the rare year four, the rest in the years two and three. The shekels bore, on one side, the form of a chalice or goblet and around it the inscription in archaic Hebrew *Shekel of Israel;* the other side showed a branch with three flowers and the inscription *Jerusalem the Holy.* The half-shekels had the same emblems, the same Jerusalem inscription on one side, but the other bore the words *Half a Shekel.* All were marked with the number of the year in which they had been struck.

Several weeks later, the expedition turned up a smaller hoard of similar coins nearby—six shekels and six half-shekels, inside a bronze box. These were found in a layer of ashes and had also been hidden by the Zealots.

Earlier, in a chamber of the casemate wall, a hoard of seventeen silver shekels, ranging through all five years of the revolt, had been found. Among them were three which had been struck in the year five. *Year Five* coins are the rarest of all. Until this find, only six such coins were known to exist in the world.

This is the first time in the history of an archaeological excavation that scholars have come across shekels; the first time that so many have been found on one site; and the only time that they have been discovered in a stratum which can be definitely dated to the period of the Jewish War against the Romans. This offers final proof that shekels with such markings belonged to this period. Since their date-mark was simply *Year One* or *Year Two* and so on, some scholars had disputed the generally held view that they had been struck during the revolt. This find put an end to the argument.

5 · THE REMAINS
OF THE ZEALOTS

The Wall

There had been significant finds of Zealot remains in the other Herodian buildings; but it was the rich Zealot discoveries in the casemate wall that enable us today to recapture the life and spirit of their time on Masada. We now know exactly where on Masada they dwelt, how they lived, how they were organized, how they fought their besiegers, what ammunition they used, how they followed their orthodox religious practices—and even what they did in the few minutes before their bitter end.

It was in the casemate wall that the expedition found not only the small items from which the scholar is able to piece together the pattern of living in ancient periods, such as sherds and complete vessels, cooking stoves, coins, implements, leather and cloth fragments, but also ruins of Zealot buildings. Of these, the discoveries of the highest importance were those of the Zealot synagogue—which makes it the most ancient synagogue in existence—and a Jewish ritual bath, also the earliest on record. In the wall, too, they discovered what every archaeologist hopes above all to find when he plans a dig—writings of the period. They found ancient Hebrew scrolls, some of the sacred writings which the Zealots always carried with them and must have hidden before taking their lives.

Josephus had written that Herod had fortified the top of the Masada rock with an encircling wall, and upon the wall he had erected thirty-eight towers. He gave their height and other measurements, which proved on the whole to be remarkably accurate.

Little of this was immediately visible to the casual visitor to Masada before the Yadin excavations. He would simply have seen a ridge of rubble around the perimeter. But from recent aerial photographs and brief examinations on the ground, scholars could detect unmistakable signs of a casemate wall. This type of wall was common in Herod's day, and the chambers within it were usually used for stores or as quarters for the guards. The Yadin expedition was the first to examine the casemate wall, and by the end of their second season, the diggers had completely uncovered the entire three-quarters of a mile of wall and registered their most dramatic finds.

They found that the outer and inner walls of the casemate were made of stone quarried on Masada; that they were thirteen feet apart (Josephus put this figure, namely the width of the casemate, at "eight cubits," which would be twelve feet); and that originally there had been about 110 rooms or chambers inside the wall and towers, all, naturally, the same width —thirteen feet—but varying in length.

Seeing the wall after the excavations offers little idea of how difficult the work of clearance was. No section had remained intact. Collapse had been general, some of the stones falling over the steep sides to the depths below, and some falling inwards. Moreover, the location of the ruins, on the very edge of the almost vertical slopes, made excavation and restoration

*A section of the western casemate wall. Top left are ruins of the Byzan-
tine chapel. Top right, the storerooms.*

The staggered stone "bricks" at left of picture are part of a tower built in Herod's time at the western part of the casemate wall, just above where the Romans later built the ramp. At right of photo is part of interior wall added by Byzantine monks.

Niche in the inner wall of the southeast section of the casemate wall.

rather dangerous. Everyone had to be very careful, and the work here went more slowly than elsewhere; but the danger added to the excitement, and when the rewards began to show up from beneath the debris, the casemate wall became a coveted assignment for the volunteers.

The excavations showed that the wall had been the principal "housing estate" of the Zealots, its rooms serving as their main dwelling quarters. The original 110 had been multiplied by the addition of partition walls which divided the larger chambers into small rooms serving one or more families. The teams found that the Zealots had also installed such domestic items as closets and mud ovens. The contrast between these small partitioned rooms, some no larger than cubicles, with their primitively built additions, and the luxury of the palace-villa and the bathhouse, made very real the difference between the circumstances of the Zealots and those of Herod and his retainers.

When the excavators got down to floor level, they came across sherds of numerous vessels—jugs, jars, bowls, mugs, cooking pots, oil lamps (some of them made of soft stone)— literally hundreds of bronze coins belonging to the period of the Jewish revolt, most of them found on the floor; and bits of cloth, woven from wool, showing very fine workmanship, representing, in the words of Yadin, "the earliest and most complete collection of textile material from the Roman period discovered so far."

The most touching find in many rooms, however, was something that suddenly brought to life for the twentieth century diggers the dramatic scene and mood of that last tragic night for the Zealot defenders: a small pile of ashes in a corner of the dwelling with the remains of the personal belongings of the family. Before submitting themselves to death, they had not set fire to their rooms in the casemate wall as they had to the other buildings on the summit. Their dwellings had been too humble to be of any worth to the Roman conquerors.

Ovens in a Zealot room within the western casemate wall. The size and shape of the ovens suggest that this may have been a bakery.

A part of the western section of the casemate wall, which is believed to have been turned into a tannery in the time of the Zealots.

What they had done, however, perhaps more as a symbolic act than to deny anything of value to their enemy, was to assemble their personal effects and burn them. The feelings of the Israelis in charge of the expedition at the discovery of these remains of their Zealot forbears may be gleaned from the words of Yadin:

There were rooms we excavated which at first glance had not been burnt, but we would find in a corner a heap of spent embers containing the remains of clothing, sandals, domestic utensils, and cosmetic items, which told the poignant story of how, perhaps only minutes before the end, each family had collected together its humble belongings and set them on fire. This also is how Josephus describes what happened. These small heaps of embers were perhaps the sights that moved us most during our excavation.

There were similar finds in primitive huts which the Zealots had hurriedly built on the summit as additional dwellings, and which were subjected, also for the first time, to a thorough examination by the expedition.

Although its rooms were used as living quarters, the case-mate wall played its natural role in the Zealots' defense of Masada, and the archaeological discoveries offered clues to the defensive tactics they had used. The obvious purpose of the wall, built on the very edge of the entire perimeter, was to prevent the entry of the enemy. If anyone tried to scale the steep slopes, defenders on the walls could discourage them with heavy stones or boiling oil. This meant that the roofs of the casemate rooms would serve as platforms for the defenders. It is also possible that upon them might have been built para-pets, to shield the defenders, with gaps through which they could fire their arrows and roll their stones.

While the whole wall would be guarded, it could be sup-posed that Eleazar ben Ya'ir, during the siege, would have posted especially strong units along those sections where an entry attempt was likely. With his limited manpower, he

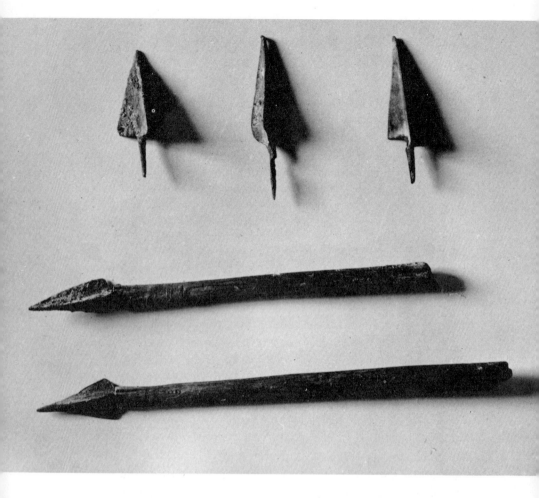

Arrows and arrowheads used by the Zealots in their last ditch defense.

might have assigned only individual lookouts, to give the signal in case of danger, to those parts of the wall that overlooked the steepest slopes. He would concentrate his forces on the battlements that lay directly above the easiest approaches to the summit, like the snake path on the eastern slope, the "White Cliff" on the western slope, and other slopes where the climb was difficult but not impossible. Clearly, with the building of the Roman ramp on the "White Cliff," he would have assembled most of the defenders on the western battlements. But he would not have left the other sections of the wall exposed, in case the ramp was a 'feint' and the real attack came from the east.

That this was how Ben Ya'ir had reasoned and that this was his defensive plan, were proved by the finds. On the floors of rooms along key sections of the casemate wall, notably above the snake path, were discovered small stocks of Zealot "ammunition"—large round one-hundred-pound stones. This suggested that they had been piled on the platforms of the wall, namely, above the roofs of the casemate rooms, and had fallen through to the floors when the roofs collapsed. They had not been used because the final attack had not come from these directions, although it is possible that early in the siege there had been attempted assaults here which had been repulsed with the aid of earlier piles of stones.

The final Roman attack had been concentrated on one section of the wall—in the west, above the ramp. Here the expedition found not Zealot ammunition—they must have expended every stone they had there—but plenty of Roman missiles, hurled from their catapults against the defenders. These missiles were round stones, "the size of grapefruit," and hundreds were discovered beneath the debris in this part of the casemate wall. Standing on the wall, glancing down at the Roman ramp, and after having examined the rival missiles, it was not difficult for the diggers to conjure up that first century battle scene and to capture the spirit of that valiant few who stood firm to the end against the might of the many.

The House of Worship

The expedition had started digging in the northwestern section of the casemate wall, overlooking the Roman camp of General Silva, at the beginning of the first season. They had quickly seen that one structure here was different from the other chambers in the casemate. It was clearly a rectangular building, but only part of it, the western portion, fitted into the wall. Its eastern section extended onto the summit. It was obviously something special; but what?

Then, as the first layers of debris were removed, there came into view a bench running around the walls of what appeared to be a large hall. What could this mean?

They dug further and found that beneath the top bench was another. When they reached floor level, they found that there were four such benches, seating tiers, looking like broad flights of steps against each wall. The eastern wall had an entrance gap in the center. Part of the western wall obtruded into the hall, and that part was without benches. It belonged to the northwestern corner of the building, which had been partitioned off into a cubicle. From the floor of the hall rose five broken columns, two in front of the northern benches and three in front of the southern.

Coins belonging to the period of the Jewish revolt were found scattered on the floor, so it was evident that this site had been used by the Zealots. When the archaeologists examined the building materials beneath the plaster on the benches, they found that some of the stones had been taken from Herodian buildings elsewhere on Masada. Notable among them were sections of columns and capitals recognizable as having come from Herod's palace-villa. This meant that the benches had been installed by the Zealots after there had been some destruction of the villa.

With this in mind, and looking at the now exposed ruins, the archaeologists reasoned as follows: the tiers of benches obviously suggested seating places for a gathering of the public. The presence of the columns pointed to the hall as being a special public meeting place. It had been constructed by the Zealots. Now why would the Zealots have gone to the trouble of building this hall? They had had little time and little taste for unnecessary luxuries. If Eleazar ben Ya'ir had wanted a communal gathering, it could have been held in the open or in one of the larger rooms in any of the existing buildings.

The archaeologists then asked themselves: what, in general, would have prompted the Zealots to expend time and energy on structural additions? They would have done so for three purposes—defense, religion, housing. The hall they had just excavated had no security function. Nor did it suit the needs of a dwelling. But a meeting place for religious purposes—a house of worship—that made sense. The construction of a synagogue, a special communal hall for prayer, would have been a most fitting act of deeply orthodox religious Jews, which the Zealots were.

The building was oriented toward Jerusalem. From earliest times, wherever the Jews lived, the traditional orientation of their synagogue was toward Jerusalem. To this very day, in any synagogue in the world, this tradition is followed.

Among the finds on the floor, apart from the coins, was a sherd with the Hebrew inscription *priestly tithe*. This on its own did not prove that the hall was a synagogue, but its religious association could be of relevance. Numerous oil lamps were found in one corner, their outer surface blackened by fire. On the floor of the cubicle were obvious remains of

Original benches and pillars of the Masada synagogue, the oldest in the world.

deliberate burning, vessels and furniture having clearly been gathered together in a heap and set ablaze.

Throughout the entire first season of excavations, Yadin harbored the feeling that it was the Zealots' synagogue. He was reluctant to be more positive, because he did not think the physical evidence, important though it was, was sufficiently weighty to prove beyond doubt the accuracy of his reasoning. But scholars were greatly intrigued by his theory, and there seemed to be no loopholes.

It caused quite a lot of excitement in Israel, for up until then, the most ancient synagogues discovered by archaeologists in the country belonged to the end of the second century. If this Masada building was indeed a synagogue, its date could be no later than the third quarter of the first century.

It was with considerable enthusiasm that the expedition continued the dig on this site with the opening of the second season. There had already been signs at the end of the first that the Zealots had built on the foundations of an earlier structure, and this was now confirmed. The building was Herodian. It followed the same overall outline as the Zealotian structure, but there were four major differences in the internal arrangements. It had no benches; there was no cubicle; the arrangement of the columns was different; and there had been an additional wall, also with a gap in the center, dividing the hall into a main room and an entrance hall.

The Zealots had added the cubicle and the benches, laid a new floor, and removed the dividing wall. In putting up the cubicle, they had had to remove two of the columns, and these were placed where the dividing wall had been. Yadin suggests that it had probably served as a synagogue in Herod's day.

The excavations continued, and a treasured prize came to light beneath the Zealot floor of the cubicle—a scroll! Yadin examined it where it lay, before its removal, and he saw that it had not been flung there at random. It had been deliberately placed in the very position in which it was found. The Zealots had cut a hole in the floor, put the scroll at the bottom, and refilled the hole with earth and stones.

Why had they hidden it? Either they hid it to keep it from the Romans, or they buried it because it was no longer in use. We have seen, in an earlier chapter, that material bearing sacred Hebrew writing was never thrown away or destroyed but buried in consecrated ground.

Ancient scrolls, particularly when first exposed to the atmosphere after nineteen hundred years, need to be handled with extreme care. The happy volunteer finders had to wait until their scroll was opened in a laboratory in Jerusalem before they found out that what they had discovered was the last two chapters of the Old Testament *Book of Deuteronomy*! The text is almost identical with the Hebrew text of *Deuteronomy* read today in the synagogue.

After this find, Yadin gave instructions that the entire floor of the cubicle be excavated to see if there were any more such "scroll holes." Sure enough, another pit was found, its earth filling different in texture from the surrounding earth and debris. It had evidently been tamped down. Beneath it lay the remains of another scroll, which turned out to be portions of the *Book of Ezekiel*. Here, too, the text is almost the same as the modern Hebrew text of this Old Testament prophet.

The discovery of these scrolls and their burial in this location, taken together with the additional evidence, do much to support Yadin's reasoning that here indeed was the synagogue of Masada, the most ancient in the world.

The Mikve

Across the way from the synagogue, on the other side of the summit, the archaeologists excavating the southeastern section of the casemate wall discovered another construction that was also different from the chambers the Zealots had used as dwellings. Here, too, the Zealots had made changes in the original Herodian building for a special—a religious—purpose. When all the debris was cleared and the structure was fully exposed, it was so well-preserved that it looked much as it must have looked in the first century.

At first glance there seemed to be nothing spectacular about it. In place of the usual chamber in the casemate were what looked like three small roughly rectangular cisterns, varying in size. There was a small hole in the partition wall dividing the largest and the middle-sized cisterns, and it was evident that it had been deliberately put there when the wall was built. It was no accidental perforation. This hole was to serve the scholars as a key clue to the function of the building.

In each of these two larger cisterns there were steps leading to the bottom. The smallest cistern of the three adjoined the middle-sized one, an intact wall between them. Leading into the largest cistern from the outside was a plastered duct or open pipe.

That was all.

What was so important about these cisterns, the hole, the duct, the steps, and why did their discovery cause such excitement among the diggers of the Yadin expedition?

To understand the significance of this archaeological find, one must know a little about religious customs and ritual of the times, particularly the practice of ritual ablution. It was this knowledge, as soon as the hole and the duct had come to light, that prompted Yadin to conclude that what was being excavated was the ritual bath of the Zealots, known in Hebrew as the *mikve*. When the dig was completed and the cisterns measured and examined by the archaeologists, as well as by religious scholars, it was seen beyond doubt that this was indeed a *mikve*, the only one ever discovered belonging to such early times.

The custom of ablution, dipping part or all of the body in water in accordance with specially prescribed religious instructions, has been—and still is—common to many religions. It is both a physical and symbolic act of cleansing and purification. The Hindu is expected to take a ceremonial bath before his daily act of worship. Baptism is a Christian ritual ablution. Orthodox Jews to this day immerse themselves in a *mikve* on prescribed occasions.

The ancient codes of these and other religions laid down very careful regulations as to how the ritual was to be performed. It was not like the normal casual act of washing. It was a very strict procedure. Nevertheless, in the hot Middle East, which was the birthplace of Judaism, Christianity, and Islam, there were special dispensations in times of water scarcity. A devout Moslem Bedouin in the desert, for example, who was supposed to wash hands, feet, and face before his daily prayers, was allowed to use sand when he was far from a source of water.

The Jewish code also took account of water shortages in Israel, although it did not go so far in its exemptions. Under normal conditions, ritual water for a *mikve* mainly had to be rainwater flowing directly into the bath or pool or cistern. It could not be drawn water, that is, water brought in containers from some other source and poured into the ritual pool, presumably because of the danger of contamination from impure vessels. However, as parts of Israel, like Masada, have no rain for most of the year and receive very little even during the rainy season, the code offered the following rule: ordinary water could be used in a *mikve* provided some drops of rainwater were added by direct flow. Contact with the "pure" water would thus symbolically purify the whole.

The ancient rabbis had also recorded how this was to be done, but some of these instructions were obscure to modern scholars of the *Mishna*—the name of the Jewish code—until the Yadin discovery, and then everything became clear.

The largest cistern stored rainwater which it received by direct flow from the open duct; the duct channeled into it the rainwater which collected on the roof during the "wet" season.

The middle-sized cistern was really the *mikve* proper, the bath or pool where immersion took place. This would be filled by drawn water. Just before use, the stopper would be removed from the hole in the dividing wall between this pool and the large cistern to allow some of the pure rainwater to trickle through. This system of storage and rationing and direct flow of the precious "pure" water enabled the *mikve* to meet the ritual demands throughout the long dry months at Masada.

The smallest of the three cisterns had no ritual function; it served merely as a place for the washing of hands and feet before the bather entered the *mikve*.

Much later in the excavations, the archaeologists found another *mikve*, which followed the same three-pool and purification system as this one, in the court of the administration building near the storerooms in the northern section of the summit.

We can now understand why this discovery by the Yadin expedition is of importance to archaeologists, and also—perhaps more so—to scholars of the *Mishna* and the *Talmud*. The *Mishna*, as we have said, is the codification of traditional Jewish laws, while the *Talmud* is the vast and comprehensive commentary on the *Mishna*, embracing the early wisdom, written and oral, of the Jewish people. The compilation of the *Mishna* was a long process which was completed at the end of the second century A.D., that is, about 130 years after the fateful events at Masada. The laws and regulations, however, were in being before they were assembled into the Mishnaic code. The *mikve* discovery at Masada offers one of those extremely rare opportunities to scholars to clarify what those laws were; to see how they were respected by orthodox Jews in the pre-Mishnaic period; and also to match them with and find the meaning of hitherto obscure passages in the regulations as they finally appeared in the *Mishna*.

It is evident from such studies that there was almost no change. It is equally evident that the devoutness of the Masada Zealots extended to a meticulous adherence to the most minute instruction of Jewish religious law concerning ritual bathing. In view of the location of Masada and the circumstances of the Zealots, such observance must be counted a supreme triumph over the harshest of odds.

The Ancient Writings

It was the earnest hope of the expedition before they started digging that they would turn up written material of the Zealot period. By the end of the second season, they had discovered some seven hundred ostraca, pieces of broken pottery vessels bearing inscriptions, and, rarest and most prized of all, portions of no less than fourteen scrolls. Two, as we have seen, were found hidden beneath the floor of the synagogue. One was discovered beneath the rubble covering the large wall behind the palace-villa. One was unearthed in a tower in the casemate wall near the western palace after nine feet of debris had been removed. All the remaining ten scrolls were found in chambers in the wall.

For students of paleography (the study of ancient writings and inscriptions), for students of the literature of the period, and for historians of religious thought at the time, these discoveries are of front rank importance.

Most of the ostraca were of the Zealot period, and the writing was in Hebrew. We have already mentioned some referring to priestly tithes. Others bore Jewish names which may have been those of Zealot commanders. Almost three hundred, which were found near the storerooms, were marked with one, two, or three Hebrew letters, and Yadin suggests that they may have been used in the Zealot rationing system during the siege. A study of the writing on these ostraca sheds much light on the development of the Hebrew script.

There were several, however, which belonged to the period of Herod. The expedition was fortunate to find some marked with a date—a very rare archaeological occurrence. The ostraca were parts of jars containing wine which had been sent from Italy. The date was recorded in the usual Roman way by reference to the man who was Roman consul that year. The name on these jars was C. Sentius Saturninus, who was consul in the year 19 B.C.

The jars also bore an inscription which read: *To King Herod of Judea*. Finding the written name of a known personage is also extremely rare in an archaeological dig. If there had been no record by Josephus, this discovery alone might have been a key clue to Herod's association with Masada. It was the first time on Masada that an inscription with Herod's name had been found.

The finds of ostraca in general are not at all uncommon in an archaeological dig, as we already know, for pottery is hard and durable. The find of an ancient scroll, anywhere, is, however, most unusual, for parchment and papyrus disintegrate with time. If weather does not do the job of destruction, insects and animals do. So far, scrolls have been found only in caves, in hot and dry regions like the Dead Sea area. At Masada, for the first time in archaeological history, parchment scrolls were found among ruined buildings in an archaeological level which it was possible to date with accuracy.

The importance of this is perhaps worth a few words of explanation. The most famous ancient scrolls with which the public is familiar are the Dead Sea Scrolls. The seven complete scrolls, now on permanent view in the Israel Museum, Jerusalem, were found in 1947 when some Bedouin goatherds, searching for a stray goat, came upon an opening in the rocks overlooking the shores of the Dead Sea. Idly throwing stones into the natural cavern, they were surprised to hear an unusual sound. The stones had hit pottery. Still worried about their missing goat, they left the spot but returned the next day to investigate. Entering the cave, they found several earthenware jars. Inside them were bundles of leather, some wrapped in linen. These were the scrolls, which then began their adventurous journey—first through the commercial hands of antique dealers and then through the scholarly hands of scientific researchers. As a matter of fact it was Yadin's father, the late Professor Elazar L. Sukenik, who was the first scholar to see the scrolls and to identify them for what they were.

The scrolls were subjected to a great deal of study which has produced a vast literature of scholarship, and today almost all experts agree that while their date cannot be pinpointed, they belong to either the first century B.C. or the first half of the first century A.D. But while the research continued, a few scholars suggested that the date was much later, and one went on record with the extreme view that they may even have been as late as the Middle Ages.

Now, such an extreme view might never have been uttered if the scrolls had not been found in a cave. For a natural cave is, to all intents and purposes, timeless, formed by some violent event in nature tens or even hundreds of thousands of years ago. A skeptic could thus claim—if it were not for additional evidence to the contrary—that the scrolls may have been placed in the cave at any time in the past, either 300 or 3,000 years ago. Scholars of the majority view had therefore to bring supporting proof to back their theories, which they did by reference to the written script, the shape of the letters, the content, the style, as well as to the parchment, the linen wrapping, the shape and make of the pottery containers, and numerous other items of evidence.

At Masada, however, most of the scrolls were found on the floors of buildings which could be dated not later than the end of the first century B.C. Two of them were found *beneath* the floor of the synagogue which the Zealots had added, so they could not be later than A.D. 73 and were most certainly earlier. Moreover, on top of some of them lay bronze coins dating to year two and year three of the Jewish revolt. Incidentally, one of the scrolls is similar to a Dead Sea Scroll found in the vicinity of the 1947 cave, so indirectly the Masada discoveries confirm the antiquity of the Dead Sea Scrolls and put a final end to the minority objection.

It should be recalled that Masada is less than thirty miles away, to the south, of Qumran, the site of the caves where the first Dead Sea Scrolls were found.

Now to the Masada scrolls themselves. Most of them were biblical. In addition to the parts of *Deuteronomy* and *Ezekiel* found in the synagogue, there were two containing several chapters of *Leviticus* and two with chapters of the *Book of Psalms*. Their texts are almost identical with the Hebrew biblical texts in use today. The differences are very minor. The *Psalms of David* as recited in today's synagogues are the same as those uttered by the Zealots in their synagogue—the same Hebrew words, the same sentence structure, the same beginning and end of each chapter.

This may not seem odd to us now, because we live in a world of books and printing; but there was no printing in those days. Everything was copied—with all the possibilities for mistakes that hand copying entails. Moreover, in those days, too, there was no punctuation to the biblical texts, no commas, no periods to denote the end of a sentence, no capital letters (this is true of modern Hebrew, too) to indicate the beginning of a sentence; and written Hebrew has no vowels. The Hebrew punctuation and vowel system was introduced only in the eighth century A.D.

The correct pronunciation and punctuation of a text was entirely determined by its meaning. For example, a word of three consonants—since there were no written vowels—might be pronounced in five or more different ways, each with a different meaning. Only one would be correct, but there might be a second that would be feasible and also make sense, although not the intended sense. As an exercise in how difficult this can be, try discovering the sense of an English word if you are given only its three consonants, like b r d. It could be bird, bard, bored, broad, bride, braid, barred, breed, bred. You can probably think of others. You would probably grasp the correct one from the context; but remember that the other words in the sentence would also be capable of more than one pronunciation and meaning.

Nonetheless, with all the opportunities for distortions and obscurities in time, there is no change in the Hebrew texts used today from those used by the Zealots, despite the gap of some 2,000 years. This shows how firm and how faithful was the tradition of Judaism. The correct text and the correct way of reading the Bible were handed down from father to son, from rabbi to student, with extreme accuracy throughout the generations.

One of the non-biblical texts, which was found in the same room in the casemate wall which yielded the seventeen silver shekels, was identical with the text of a scroll found in one of the Dead Sea caves. It contained *the Songs of the Sabbath Sacrifices,* and dealt with the Sabbath ritual of the Jewish Dead Sea sect, who followed their own special calendar and who had broken with the Jewish religious authorities in the land. The presence of such a scroll does not mean that the Zealots belonged to this sect. Yadin points out that it is known that some members of the sect took part in the Jewish revolt and a few probably joined the Zealots at Masada after the fall of Jerusalem to continue resistance to the Romans. They would naturally have taken their sacred scrolls with them.

The scroll found in the wall tower turned out to be the *Book of Jubilees* in its original Hebrew text. To understand the importance of this find, we have to go back to early times and know a little about the religious writings from which the final selection was made of those formally accepted as books of the Bible. This official list of books of Scripture is known as the canon. There is thus the canon of the Old Testament and, very much later, the canon of the New Testament.

From about the sixth century B.C. onwards, maybe earlier, the Old Testament canon was gradually evolving. In the centuries that followed, right up to the end of the first century A.D., there were various collections of sacred writings—apart from the *Five Books of Moses* (the *Pentateuch*), the *Prophets,* and the other books which were subsequently included in the Bible—which were also held by the Jews to be holy. Only about A.D. 90 or 100 was the final canon of the Old Testament determined, at the great assembly of rabbis under the famed Rabbi Akiva at the religious center of Yavne near the Mediterranean coast a few miles south of today's Tel-Aviv. With the fall of Jerusalem in A.D. 70 and the rise of the Christian faith, the Jews felt the urgent need to define precisely the limits of their Bible. The books they decided on were the ones we read in our Old Testament today.

What of the books that were rejected at Yavne? They fall into two groups. The most important, namely the ones that just missed inclusion in the canon, form what is known as the Old Testament *Apocrypha*. The word *apocrypha* is the plural of the Greek *apocryphon* which means "hidden away," although such books were never really "hidden away" in the sense of being read in secret or kept from the public. Much earlier, however, when the Old Testament was translated into Greek, the books which eventually made up the *Apocrypha* were included. This first translation of the Hebrew Bible was undertaken in Alexandria, and is known as the *Septuagint.* The work took about one hundred years, from the third to the second century B.C. It is called the *Septuagint* because it was believed to have been translated by seventy-two (although *septuagint* is Latin for seventy) scribes who were divinely inspired. Initiators of the translation were the members of the large Jewish community in Alexandria who, being outside the Land of Israel, were fearful of becoming estranged from Hebrew and their Jewish faith. Greek was the language spoken in Alexandria and thus, the *Septuagint* would enable their children to read the Bible of their faith.

The inclusion of the *Apocrypha* in the *Septuagint* happened of course, much earlier than the Yavne decision on the canon. It shows, however, how highly regarded were these books in Hebrew antiquity. After they were dropped from the canon, they no longer appeared in Hebrew. But they continued to be held sacred by the Christians, and when, centuries later, the Christian canon was laid down, the Old Testament *plus* the Old Testament *Apocrypha* were included. The apocryphal texts thus came down to us not in Hebrew but in translation, notably in the Greek.

One more item of background, and we can return to Masada. We mentioned two groups of books that were excluded from the canon, the first being the *Apocrypha*. The second group was of lesser importance and known as *Pseudepigrapha*, meaning "false writings," also a Greek word. The term, applied of course much later, no doubt was meant to underline the reason for their rejection at Yavne as not having been divinely inspired; but up to the time of the Yavne assembly, such Hebrew books were considered as minor sacred works by some Jews.

After Yavne, they disappeared even more quickly than the *Apocrypha* in their Hebrew original, and those that were preserved were preserved in translations.

The *Book of Jubilees*, found by the Yadin expedition in the tower of the casemate wall at Masada, was the most important book in the *Pseudepigrapha*. It was written in the latter part of the second century B.C., in the time of the Maccabees. It is the oldest known commentary on, and an enlarged narration of, *Genesis* and the first fourteen chapters of *Exodus*. Its title comes from the term given to the fiftieth year—jubilee; for the book divides the history of the world, from the creation to the giving of the Law to Moses on Mount Sinai, into jubilee periods of forty-nine years each. It has come down to us in translation, parts of it in Greek and Latin, and a complete version in Ethiopic. The portions discovered at Masada are, it will be recalled, in the original Hebrew.

We now come to the outstanding non-biblical scroll found at Masada, more important than the pseudepigraphic *Book of Jubilees*. This was a book of the *Apocrypha* and far higher up on the list of sacred books considered by the rabbis at Yavne. It may indeed, in modern parlance, have "made" the "short list," failing only narrowly to be included in the *Old Testament*. This was *Ecclesiasticus* (not to be confused with the biblical book of *Ecclesiastes*), and the portions discovered by the Yadin expedition were in the long-lost original Hebrew text. The book, in Hebrew, is known as *The Wisdom of Ben-Sira*.

Its discovery was accompanied by a fascinating story of scholarly deduction. But first a word about the find and the content of the book.

In the debris near the floor of a room in the casemate wall just south of the gate above the snake path, the diggers came across twisted fragments of a scroll. None of the writing could be read with the naked eye. But after the scroll had been carefully treated in the Jerusalem laboratory, opened, smoothed, and photographed by the infrared process, each letter became sharply visible. After reading only a few of the Hebrew sentences, Yadin promptly recognized the work as *The Wisdom of Ben-Sira*.

Ecclesiasticus was written by Ben-Sira at the beginning of the second century B.C., and although it was later excluded from the Hebrew canon, it was highly esteemed by the rabbinical sages, and allusions to and quotations from it by the rabbis are recorded in the subsequent *Talmud*. It is a book in the tradition of the old Hebrew wisdom literature, and commentators have pointed to the influence on Ben-Sira of the biblical *Book of Proverbs*. It sings the praises of the wise and righteous men of ancient Israel, presents wisdom as a revelation of God and as a guide to conduct, and tells of the rewards of the study of wisdom. Its moral themes are written in the form of proverbs.

The Wisdom of Ben-Sira was translated from the original Hebrew into Greek by Ben-Sira's grandson in the latter half of the second century B.C. Accepted at the time as part of their Scriptures by the Jews of Alexandria, it was included in the *Septuagint* and thus passed on to the Christian church. Except for the *Psalms of David*, it is the most widely used Old Testament work in the Roman Catholic liturgy.

After the Yavne decision on the Jewish canon, the original Hebrew text dropped out of sight until fairly recently, and throughout the centuries, the Greek version was considered the standard text.

Then, in 1896, something startling happened—startling in the world of scholarship. In that year, an old and forgotten archive was discovered in a neglected loft of the ancient Ezra Synagogue of Old Cairo, which had been founded in the year 882. This loft, a room without doors or windows in the rear of the building, was reached by climbing a ladder and entering through a hole in the wall. It turned out to be the synagogue *Geniza*. *Geniza* is the Hebrew word for "hidden away" —like the Greek word *apocryphon*—and has come to mean both the hiding place and the item hidden. The purpose of this hiding place—really a special storage place—was to store old Hebrew books and writings no longer in use to await burial in consecrated ground. The Jews would thus deposit written and printed material in the *Geniza* provided by the synagogue, so that they would not be profaned by misuse, and every so often they would be taken away for burial.

In the course of time, the Cairo *Geniza* seems to have been forgotten, and so the fragments of handwritten manuscripts and printed books, documents, and letters just lay there undisturbed for several hundred years. During the last century, however, it was rediscovered, and several visitors managed to acquire a number of manuscripts. The most notable was a Russian Jew named Abraham Firkowitch, who assembled the largest collection of Hebrew manuscripts in the world, a collection acquired by the Leningrad Library in the 1870's.

In 1896, two learned Scottish ladies, who lived in Cambridge, England, were on a trip to the Middle East and in Cairo bought some fragments which had come from the *Geniza*. On their return to Cambridge, they presented two leaves with Hebrew writing, one of parchment and one of paper, to Solomon Schechter, who was then Reader (Associate Professor) of Talmudic Studies at Cambridge University. The parchment, he quickly saw, was part of a manuscript of the Palestinian *Talmud*. The Hebrew text on the paper fragment, he discovered after some study, belonged to—*Ecclesiasticus, The Wisdom of Joshua Ben-Sira!*

Schechter thus found himself staring at a fragment of a book whose original Hebrew text had been lost for many centuries. It was clear to him that where one leaf had been found, more leaves and perhaps other important material might also be found. The sensational discovery sent a thrill through the normally sober and quiet university city, and it was decided to send Schechter to Cairo to try and bring back to Cambridge whatever he could find in the *Geniza*.

Schechter went, under the auspices of the university, and also armed with a letter of introduction to the Chief Rabbi in Cairo, Raphael ben Shimon, who proved most helpful. He allowed Schechter into the *Geniza* and told him he could take away, free, whatever he wished. Schechter spent several weeks in the dark and musty room and at the end assembled for removal to Cambridge only the handwritten manuscripts.

This treasury is so rich that to this day there are manuscripts which still await thorough study. But among the early ones sorted out and examined and published were parts of our by now familiar *Ecclesiasticus*. Indeed, when Cambridge University made its official announcement of the gift in June 1898, offering its thanks to "the heads of the Cairo Jewish community," they singled out this manuscript for special mention: "Among the more noteworthy treasures which this Collection contains are fragments of the *Book of Ecclesiasticus* in Hebrew. . . ."

Recalling that this book had been preserved only in translation, you may have been wondering how it was that Yadin, "after reading only a few of the Hebrew sentences" of the scroll found at Masada, "promptly recognized the work." Now you have the clue. Yadin had remembered the Hebrew from the *Geniza* text published by Schechter.

But that is not quite the end of the story. After the Schechter publication, a hot argument broke out among scholars over the date of the *Geniza* text. The majority maintained that this was in fact a copy made in the Middle Ages of the original Ben-Sira Hebrew. There may have been some minor errors. This would have been natural in a medieval copy inscribed anywhere from 1,000 to 1,500 years after the issue of the original. But they firmly held that it was a direct copy of the Hebrew original. There were, however, a few scholars who argued that this text was a medieval Hebrew translation of the Greek or Syriac translation of the original Hebrew! (The Syriac version had been made directly from the Hebrew in about A.D. 200.)

Since no Hebrew text existed which could be definitely proved to be an authentic copy of the original and against which the *Geniza* text could be matched, the argument had to be left open, each scholar holding to his point of view.

Then came the discovery at Masada. The scroll was clearly not medieval but very close in time to the period when *The Wisdom of Ben-Sira* was written. It was indeed a portion of the original Hebrew text. With great eagerness Yadin hastened to compare it with the *Geniza* text. The result put an end to the seventy-year-old argument. The two texts were basically identical.

As Yadin writes: "The text in the Cairo *Geniza* on the whole represents the original Ben-Sira Hebrew text. I say 'on the whole' because there are, of course, some corruptions, some earlier, some later, some the fault of copyists. . . . But the model was clearly the original Ben-Sira."

He concludes: "Our discovery may have stopped the controversy over, but not the study of, Ben-Sira. Indeed it has opened a new chapter in research on this book, which is one of the most important apocryphal works and one of the greatest Hebrew books of the period of the Second Temple."

The Most Dramatic Find

Throughout the excavations at Masada, the story of the Zealots' last stand was always in the minds of the archaeologists. As the volunteers dug and the professionals evaluated, the archaeological worth of whatever ruin or object was being exposed was, of course, of immediate interest. But what might be called their "Zealot antenna" was always out, sensing whether the finds could be related to the details they remembered in the record of Josephus.

One day, the teams were going about their normal business in the northern section of Masada at what must have been a key site in ancient days. It was close to the storerooms, the administration building, the Roman-style bathhouse, and a gate in the casemate wall. They dug, they scraped, and they sifted the debris, inspecting the items that had been left at the top of the sieve. Nothing sensational had been found that day, just routine sherds—although whether they were "routine" or bore marks of writing would be known only after they were washed. The sherds were put in pails, the pails tagged with the markings of the level and the site, and sent below.

When they returned to camp after the day's dig, this particular volunteer group learned that they had discovered what would turn out to be the most dramatic find on Masada. Not a discovery of vital importance to archaeology. Not one which would revolutionize theories of scholarship. But a find dramatic in human terms, one that would move all who were familiar with the touching story of the Zealots.

The discovery consisted of eleven ostraca. That, in itself, was not startling. But these were different from the usual run of pieces of pottery bearing inscriptions. They were all about the same size, quite small; each bore Hebrew letters, making up a single word; the word was a name; the name on each was different; and some of the names were clearly nicknames, like "the hunter."

Yadin stared at these ostraca for a long time, wondering what they had meant to the ancient occupants of the site. Then into his mind flashed the paragraph in Josephus that followed Eleazar ben Ya'ir's historic address to his doomed comrades. After the men had killed their wives and children,

they cast lots for the selection of ten men of their number to destroy the rest. These being chosen, the devoted victims embraced the bodies of their deceased families, and then, ranging themselves near them, cheerfully resigned themselves to the hands of the executioners. When these ten men had discharged their disagreeable task, they again cast lots as to which of the ten should kill the other nine, and last of all himself.

The simplest way of casting lots—children do it all the time in their games—is to recite a jingle and point to a different person in the group with each word. The one who gets the last word is chosen. For something serious—and at Masada the occasion could not have been more serious—the method chosen would be to write each person's name on an object, drop the objects into a vessel or some other container, and then draw one out. Today the names would be written on a piece of paper and the papers dropped into a hat. At Masada, they would be written on a piece of pottery. The eleven ostraca that were found seemed to have been inscribed by the same hand.

Were these the lots that had been used to choose the last Zealot from among the final ten who "should kill the other nine?"

The immediate problem, of course, was that there were eleven ostraca and not ten. And this is still a problem if Josephus was accurate. There can never be any certainty that these were in fact the actual lots by which the grim choice was made; but one of them was of very special interest, and its very presence suggested its use for an occasion of the highest importance. Written upon it was the name Ben Ya'ir! There was only one person who would be referred to simply as Ben Ya'ir —the commander of the Zealots on Masada himself, Eleazar ben Ya'ir. Yadin suggests that "it also seems possible that this final group were his ten commanders who had been left to the last, after the decision had been wholly carried out, and who had then cast lots amongst themselves."

Thus ended the lives of the fighters of Masada in their final stand against the Romans.

6 · THE REMAINING
SUMMIT RUINS

Although the focus of the expedition's interest had been the period between Herod and the fall of Masada, they concerned themselves with *all* the material remains they uncovered. Taking the sites we have already described, together with the remaining ruins on the summit, they were able to present the *total* history of Masada.

The excavations showed that the only active and lively period on this rock was the one already covered in this book. However, some remains were found of a much earlier time, remains of plants, mats, cloth, and pieces of pottery belonging to the period between 4000 and 3000 B.C. (This is known as the Chalcolithic [Copper-Stone] period, when man first started making pottery and using copper.) They were found in a cave near the foot of the southern slope, and Yadin says that their owners were a typical cave-dwelling community, one of many who inhabited the Judean desert in that age.

Next comes a gap of more than 2000 years to finds from the period of the Israelite kings. Bits of pottery were dug up belonging to the tenth to seventh centuries B.C. (The tenth is the century of King David and King Solomon.) But pottery was all that was found. There was no trace of any building from this period, and it is assumed that only an occasional individual stayed there at this time.

The only other pre-Herodian remains were the ones we have already recorded—the coins of King Alexander Jannai (103–76 B.C.).

Then come the remains of Herod. In the period between his death and the arrival of the Zealots, the excavations show that Masada was continuously occupied. After the Zealots, the Romans remained for some forty years. With their departure, there were no signs of settlement for more than 300 years, until the fifth to sixth centuries A.D., the Byzantine period; and the remains of this period, the youngest, may be clearly seen on the summit. Indeed, until the Yadin excavations, which have exposed many more impressive ruins, the first structure that every visitor came upon was the Byzantine church. After the sixth century, Masada was abandoned and never again occupied.

The excavations enabled the archaeologists to piece together the history of the site during the Byzantine period. It was common, in the fifth century, for small hermit groups of Christians to seek out places of retreat in the Judean desert, and it was probably one such group that hit on Masada as an ideal spot. It was remote and isolated, and it had caves and buildings, or at least ruins, for shelter; and they chose it as their settlement. In succeeding years it attracted others seeking the monastic life, so that later in the fifth and in the sixth centuries, Masada continued to be inhabited by such men.

The expedition found that some of them had lived in the caves. Their painted crosses were still visible on the walls. Most, however, had lived in small cells which they had constructed, and the ruins of several of these were found on the summit. Masada had been struck by an earthquake some time before, and many of the Herodian buildings had toppled.

Cells of Byzantine monks on the Masada summit about fifty yards to the east of the Byzantine chapel.

Part of a wall of the Byzantine chapel, decorated with potsherds.

When the monks came along, they built some of their cells on mounds of Herodian rubble, and these were among the first ruins the expedition came across when they started digging. They also had to do a lot of careful sorting out, first removing the debris that covered the Byzantine structures; then examining, photographing, and registering these structures; then clearing them away to get at the earlier rubble beneath; and going on digging until they came to the foundations of the first buildings on the site.

Most of the Byzantine construction was primitive; but they left one impressive monument into which they put much energy, skill, and artistic talent. This was their chapel. It stands to the immediate northeast of the western palace.

Because it had been for centuries the most prominent and least ruined building on the summit, visited and examined by all the nineteenth century explorers who got to the top, the Yadin expedition thought there would be little left for them to find. What they saw, when they began their first season of excavations, was what earlier scholars had seen. Standing, roofless, was a long hall with a well-rounded apse at its eastern end. In the center of the apse was a beautifully arched window. The high stone walls of the hall were plastered, and embedded in the plaster were small stones of pottery arranged in decorative designs. A few portions of a colored mosaic floor were found in a corner of the hall, but the rest of the mosaic—and much of the floor too—had been removed.

There was little more inside the hall itself that promised to be rewarding, but there were tall piles of rubble just outside, close to its north wall, which were worth investigating. They proved to be the ruins of chambers. One was clearly a living room, for the diggers found cupboards and washing vessels. Near it was another room, and as the teams reached one part of the floor level, they were delighted to find it covered by a colored mosaic. Carefully removing the rest of the debris, they found the mosaic was complete. But only when they had

Helicopter shot of the apse in the Byzantine chapel. The mountains of Moab in the distance.

The beautiful mosaic floor that enabled Yigael Yadin to date the chapel as belonging definitely to the fifth century.

scraped and brushed away the final film of dirt, a slow and gentle job which took several days, did they see how beautiful it was. Executed in good color, it consisted of sixteen circles set symmetrically within a decorative rectangular frame, and within each circle was an individual geometrical design or the representation of a flower, a fruit, or a plant. One circle contained a basket topped with eggs, and marked on the basket was a cross. It was from this mosaic that Yadin was able to date the Byzantine chapel as belonging definitely to the fifth century.

Our description of the ancient ruins on the summit is completed; but there remains one group of structures which played a prominent part in the Masada story. These structures were down below—the fortifications of the men who had conquered Masada but not the spirit of its zealous defenders, the men who had won the battle but who are remembered in history only through the valor of their victims. These were the ruins of the Romans.

7 · THE ROMAN FORTIFICATIONS

The acoustics on top of Masada are excellent. There is a stillness about it that would make sharply audible even the distant song of a bird. But it was more than the twittering of birds that shattered the silence on the Masada summit on a certain day in A.D. 72. It was the arrival of General Silva's legionaries and the thousands of additional troops and prisoner-slaves. Long before the Romans had fired their first arrow, the clatter and the clamor and the shouting and the din as they set up camp must have split the ears of the Zealots. From then on, even in the moments when there were no hostilities, the Masada area knew no quiet.

It must have been shortly afterwards that the Zealots awakened—if indeed they could ever sleep—to a new sound. It was the banging and the clanging and the knocking and the hammering of builders, and it came not only from the west but from several points around the base of the rock. Although at first, observing the activity through slits in the parapets above their casemate wall, they might not have fathomed what it was all about, they soon found out. What they heard and saw was the construction of the Roman fortifications, and pretty powerful and formidable they were, too.

They consisted of, as has been noted, eight rectangular camps at the feet of the steep slopes, the first of the Roman structures to be built; a circumvallation (siege wall) surrounding the base of Masada; twelve towers to strengthen one section of this wall; and—eventually—the ramp. The remains are in a good state of preservation, and they show better than most ruins in territories once controlled by the Roman Empire the character and plan of Roman siege works.

The Yadin expedition undertook no thorough excavation of these ruins. Their main interest was the Masada of Herod and the Zealots, and their principal tasks were confined to the summit. They did, though, closely inspect the Roman works so as to "get the feel" of what Eleazar ben Ya'ir had been up against, what he had faced, what might he had had to resist, and therefore what measures he would have been called upon to take. The reasoning which resulted from this inspection was most helpful to the archaeologists in recapturing the mood and actions of the besieged defenders and in identifying some of their remains.

However, they did carry out a limited excavation in one of the eight camps, the one where General Silva was quartered. Again, this was done not for the purpose of examining Roman camp planning but primarily for the light that might be shed on the summit finds. These included vessels belonging to the Roman garrison that occupied the top of Masada after the end of the siege. Yadin was anxious to compare them with the pottery which the Roman army had used in the siege camps. Nevertheless, in the course of his limited study, he was able to make some important additions to the archaeological knowledge that had been recorded by several earlier scholars. It is, however, largely through the work of these scholars that we know as much as we do about the Roman fortification system.

The remains of a Nabatean bowl of the type found both on the summit of Masada and in the Roman camps.

Silva and his engineers must have spent a good deal of time moving around the base of Masada, examining, surveying, pondering, before deciding exactly the line that was to be followed by the siege wall and the tactical points where the camps were to be erected. The section of wall strengthened by the twelve towers was in the east—for obvious reasons. It was the side of the accessible snake path. The east was also the location of three of the camps. Two camps were sited in the southwest; two in the west; and one in the north.

Six of the camps were comparatively small. Two were large, averaging about 25,000 square yards, similar in layout to the standard Roman camp, and Yadin believes that these held most of the men of the Tenth Legion. One, in the west, was the headquarters camp of General Silva. The other was in the east. Both lay outside the siege wall. So did one of the small camps in the east. The other five were like irregularly placed, rectangular, outsize links in the chain of the wall.

The camps served to house the troops, to give them protection, and to seal the siege ring around the Zealots. They were so sited as to control every topographical feature which might favor the escape of the besieged or the ascent of possible reinforcements.

As to layout, the Roman Army followed a fairly standard pattern wherever they fought, and its main characteristics may be seen in the two large camps at Masada. They were rectangular tented compounds enclosed by walls, with well-guarded gates of entry in each of the four walls. At Masada, crossing the camp from east to west and from north to south, linking each pair of facing gates, were the two main camp roads. The rows of tents were sited in rectangular blocks, and each detachment of legionaries had its own block, which was always located in the same position in whatever camp was serving as their quarters. At Masada, the tents were not pegged to the ground but rested on low walls of stone rubble about three or four feet high, although their main weight was supported by poles. The men slept and ate on stone benches inside the tent, about eight or nine to a tent. You can see the remains of these low walls and benches at Masada today.

The idea behind uniform camp arrangements by the highly disciplined Roman legions was to make the soldiers familiar with their immediate surroundings wherever they served. In a campaign, and on the move, they would often have to make "one-night stands"; but even if it were only for one night, the legion would have to set up a regular camp, erecting four earth walls, with a gate in each, the same lanes crossing the compound, the tents of each detachment in their accustomed spot, the tents of the officers opposite their units. The gates and the main internal roads, or lanes, had standard names. If a legionary were dropped into any Roman camp, he would immediately know his way around. It was a Roman boast that if the camp were only five minutes old and there was a sudden attack, the troops could form ranks in an instant, even on the darkest night, and engage the enemy.

At Masada, of course, where they were laying siege and remaining a long time, the camp installations could be permanent—permanent enough to be seen to this day! The walls were of stone, not of earth, as were the tent bases and benches. There were other buildings identifiable by their ruins and location. There was the command post with its central court. There was the three-foot-high dais where the commander stood when taking the parade of his troops. There were altars for the Roman sacrifices. There was the special place, also standard in all Roman camps, for the priests who forecast the fortunes of battle. This was known by the Latin name for "bird observatory," for the "fortune-tellers" looked for omens in the flight of birds, though also, at times, in the stars in the heavens. In the large camps at Masada Yadin also found the remains of a marketplace and a treasury.

Incidentally, even though his dig in the Roman remains was on a small scale, he was able to end yet another scholarly argument. Earlier scholars had already established that inside Silva's camp, in the northwestern corner, a small camp had been built at a later date. This was evident by the destruction of parts of the old camp in the building of the new one. Some scholars held that it was built and occupied by the Romans immediately after the capture of Masada. Others put its construction at more than two hundred years later. Yadin found that the earlier date was the correct one. All the pottery and coins he discovered on this site belonged to the closing years of the first century and the opening of the second century A.D. It was clear that this small camp was built by and housed part of the Roman garrison that remained after the fall of Masada. From this and from coins found on the summit, Yadin has concluded that the Romans continued to occupy Masada for at least forty years after the deaths of the Zealots.

Even today, after a close-up look at the fortifications or a view of them from the summit, one cannot fail to be struck by the enormous might that was mobilized to crush the small group of Zealots. Putting ourselves in the sandals of these defenders, we imagine that they must have been terrified when they saw the cohorts of their enemy approaching, thousands upon thousands, ranging themselves at the foot of the slopes; establishing themselves in fortified camps; steadily building the circumvallation; attacking the summit with their stone missiles and arrows; and then applying themselves to the construction of the ramp that foreshadowed only one climax—the final assault. Yet the behavior of the Zealots did not reflect terror nor any other weakness of spirit. True, topography was on their side. But against such Roman strength, topography could serve only to delay, not to alter, the end. We know, both from Josephus and from the archaeological finds, that the Zealots reacted from the very first with the same mood of resistance which had brought them to Masada. They coolly frustrated preliminary attempts by the Romans to scale the heights. They harassed the men engaged in building the Roman siege works. Yet inexorably the work continued. They knew the purpose of the Roman ramp and knew, too, that their efforts to hold up construction were of little avail. Nevertheless they pressed on with their vigorous defense. Even when the ramp was completed, the siege tower brought up with its armored archers, the battering ram manhandled into position, and the wall breached, the Zealots did not give up. Only when their casemate wall was ablaze, their ramparts finally open to the enemy, did they recognize the inevitable. Even then their spirits remained strong. They chose death rather than surrender and set about doing what had to be done, as Josephus recorded and as the Yadin expedition confirmed in the burned buildings and the pathetic, small piles of ashes in the corner of each dwelling room.

The Roman fortifications tell much of the power of Rome. They tell more of the power of the human spirit, as exemplified by the Zealots of Masada.

ILLUSTRATIONS

INDEX

Conder, Lieutenant, 53-54

Dale, J. B., 53
dams, 95-96
dating, archaeological
  problems of, 31-32, 75-76, 82,
    184-185, 209
  significance of, 4
Dead Sea, 60
  survey of, 53
Dunayevsky, Immanuel, 43, 55

earthquake, 124, 129, 197
Eleazar ben Ya'ir, 7-10, 15-17, 20-
    28, 31, 70, 171, 175, 194, 195,
    205
  address by, to Zealot comrades,
    25-27, 133, 194
  arrival of, at Masada, 12
  See also Zealots
excavation, 49, 51, 56, 145
  plans for, 71-72, 154
  results of, 71, 196-197
expedition of 1955-56, 68, 71, 72,
    92, 95, 99, 100, 101, 102, 123

finds, routine, 84
fire, traces of Zealots', 122-123,
    130, 133, 147, 148, 168, 171
firebrands, as weapons in siege
    against Masada, 22-24
Firkowitch, Abraham, 191
flash floods, 95, 96
fortifications
  Herod's, 8-10, 12
  Roman, 204-210

Garrison Building, 160
Gasco, Yitzhak, 51
Guttman, Shmaryahu, 46, 54, 55,
    91, 92, 99

hanging palace. See palace, hang-

ing (northern building; pal-
    ace-villa)
Herod, King, 8-10
  background of, 10-11
  buildings erected by, 66-68
  fortifications at Masada built
    by, 8-10, 12
  palaces of, 101
Historic Sites, Department for the
    Preservation of, 51

Israel Army, Yadin expedition
    aided by, 40
Israeli War of Independence, 54
Israel National Parks Authority,
    51

Jerusalem, 14, 100
Jews, antagonism of, to Herod,
    10-11
Jewish War against the Romans,
    Great, 6, 7
Jonathan the High Priest, identity
    of, 32, 124-125
Josephus, historian, 30, 32-36, 49,
    52, 53, 56, 65, 68, 69, 70, 83, 91,
    92, 97, 100, 114, 123, 124, 125,
    127, 133, 135, 164, 183, 193
  palace identification by, 72, 99,
    101, 144
  quoted, 8, 12, 18, 23, 25-27, 28-
    29, 32, 33, 34, 35, 60, 105,
    194
Judea, 6, 10, 11, 12, 14

kibbutz team, 55
  cisterns investigated by, 91-92

"levels of human settlement"
    (strata), 73-74
Livneh, Micha, 55, 99
Lynch, Lt. W. F., 53, 55, 92, 108

mikves, discovery of the, 178-181

mosaics
  in Byzantine chapel, 200-203
  in Herodian rooms, 102-103
  in Roman-style baths, 141, 143
  in throne room, 147-148
mound, upper terrace, palace-villa, 103-105

NAPHTA oil company, 42-43
northern building (on Masada)
  description of, 66
  speculation concerning, 66-68, 100-101
  See also palaces

ostraca, 84, 182-183, 194, 195

paintings
  in Herodian palace, 103, 108, 112, 114-119, 122
  in Roman-style baths, 142, 143
  in working palace, 154
palace-villa, 123-125, 154
  columns of, 105, 109-114
  terraces of, 102, 103-108, 109-112, 119-122
palaces
  hanging, 97-125
  Herod's private (palace-villa), 101-102
  western (working), 102, 144-151
Palestine Exploration Fund, 53-54
Petrie, Sir Flinders, pottery dating first used by, 81-82
photographing, 80
pottery (potsherds), 3
  as chronological clues, 80-84
  handling of, 80
  reconstruction of, 84
  Zealots', 130-132

ramp, Roman-built, 17-18, 20, 22, 61, 65, 173, 205, 209, 210

recording, importance of, 82
restoration, 49-51, 71
  of Herod's storehouses, 128-129
Robinson, Dr. Edward, 52
Romans, Great Jewish War against, 6, 7
ruins, Masada, 65, 196-203
  early descriptions of, 53, 56
ruins, Roman, 203
  See also fortifications, Roman

sacred writings, Zealots', 187-193
  Yadin's theory concerning, 68
  See also scrolls
Saulcy, F. de, 71-72
Schechter, Solomon, 191-192
Schulten, Adolf, 54, 68, 71, 144-145, 158
  palace identification by, 72, 99, 101, 144
scrolls, 164, 177-178, 182, 183
  Dead Sea, 31, 183, 185
  instructions to volunteers concerning, 68-69
  Masada, 185, 186-193
shards (sherds). See pottery
shekels of Israel, 4, 162
  See also coins
siege, Silva's, against Zealots, 16, 20
siege tower, 18, 20, 21, 23
Silva, Flavius, 100, 204
  camp occupied by, 16, 205, 207
  Masada attacked by, 14-24
skeletons, 123
Smith, E., 52
snake path, 8, 39, 53, 55, 58, 60, 92, 207
  annual hike along, 44-45
staircase
  of Herodian palace, 106, 124
  for Yadin expedition, 38, 40, 61, 66, 105-106
storerooms (storehouses), Herod's, 70-71, 125-136